Soul Signs in Love

Use the Power of Your Sun Sign
to Create a Healthy, Loving
Relationship with Your Perfect
Partner—from First Meeting
to Soul Bonding

Diane Eichenbaum

A FIRESIDE BOOK
Published by Simon & Schuster
NEW YORK LONDON TORONTO SYDNEY SINGAPORE

FIRESIDE
Rockefeller Center
1230 Avenue of the Americas
New York, NY 10020

Designed by Christine Weathersbee

Manufactured in the United States of America

1   3   5   7   9   10   8   6   4   2

Library of Congress Cataloging-in-Publication Data
Eichenbaum, Diane.
Soul signs in love : use the power of your sun sign to create
a healthy, loving relationship with your perfect partner—
from first meeting to soul bonding / Diane Eichenbaum.
           p.   cm.
1. Astrology. 2. Love—Miscellanea. 3. Mate
selection—Miscellanea.   I. Title.
BF1729.L6 E37 2001
133.5'864677—dc21   00-050297
ISBN 0-684-85777-4

In Acknowledgment of Love

Love is a transformative force, a magical state. Although it is a form of complete knowledge and insight, it is hard for us, being so emotionally affected by its wonder, to see its order or design.

I have found through the study and practice of astrology that there is a plan in everything. We have only to figure out what it is. We must learn how to read the signs made available to us and let love fit into our lives.

It is reassuring to realize that when love meets an obstacle that will not move, it does not die. Love simply changes shape and takes a different form.

This book is written not in order to encourage the control of love, but in order to enhance love. I wish to acknowledge love as our guide.

Contents

Soul Signs in Love

Legend

In his classic work of philosophy, the *Symposium,* Plato recounts a myth: Eons ago humans were perfectly round, with both sexes contained in one body.

A symbolic metaphor for the wholeness of the soul? Perhaps. But perhaps it wasn't a metaphor at all. Plato held a number of beliefs that would be scoffed at today in our techno-mad world. For example, he believed Atlantis was a real place. I think he was right about Atlantis—and I believe he was spot on about our origins as dual-sexual beings, too. It's not impossible to imagine Plato's vision of ethereal beings who incorporated both the male *and* female essences within the "bodies" of gorgeous amorphous balls. Beings that floated through time and space, observing life but not really a part of physical nature.

I believe that our spherical ancestors yearned not only to be a part of the physical world, but to be separate and apart from their "soul mates." They implored the gods to grant them their freedom, and eventually Zeus gave them their wish. Our perfect androgynous ancestors became not-as-perfect and *separate* male and female beings.

If the tremendous problems humans have finding love, keeping love, *enjoying* love, and yearning, always yearning for what we loosely call "our soul mates" is any indication, then the fulfillment of our spiritual ancestors' wish did not bring them—or us—the freedom they craved. We are undeniably free, but free in a kind of way that leaves us as spiritual amputees who will always feel the pain of a "missing limb." If it's not there anymore, why does it hurt so badly?

Here then is the catch—and there always is one, isn't there? For these early beings to become separated, they had to descend into the realm of matter. And so we find ourselves tied to the earth in endless cycles of life and death, longing for our lost partners.

The discomfort of feeling lost without a mate has been told in love stories through history. There is an inner longing in all of us to be connected to our lovers, and, at the same time, as deep a need to be separate from them. We attract others to help us define ourselves, to feel complete, and to see ourselves more clearly. We can't live with them and can't live without them. After we find out that being defined by someone else isn't real, we realize that the answer is inside; always inside and just out of reach. Our long-lost soul mates have left a signature deep within us, a signature as clear as our DNA—just waiting to be discovered and integrated into our consciousness. Then and only then can we explore, expand, and explode into the glorious beings we are who are ready to find and reconnect with our missing halves—our *chosen* soul mates in this lifetime.

Introduction:
Aquarian Age Relationships

"And let the winds of the heavens dance between you."

—Kahlil Gibran, *The Prophet*

Let's face it—the world was made for couples! Even the animals in Noah's Ark lined up two by two.

The desire to have love and an enduring partnership with someone you're mad about is one of the deepest longings you can have. A huge amount of our time is spent thinking about it, looking for it, and feeling miserable if we're not in it up to our necks and sinking fast. A lot of energy is spent trying to make it happen. If love was a practical process it would be easier, but it wouldn't be as delicious. The fantasy most people harbor is that the perfect person will appear and restore to us a feeling of wholeness like the one we had in the womb. After all, didn't you grow up believing that there is that one perfect person for everyone?

Think of all the people you've had relationships with in the past. (OK, forget *that* one right off, and get real here!) When the veil of illusion fell away and you really got to know them, *really* know them, you might have been disappointed to find out they weren't as magical as you thought. When it comes to courtship and commitment, fantasy goes just so far. Not to deny the mystery of chemistry and the beauty of deep soul connections, but there are deeper processes at work when it comes to finding the person to whom you want to commit yourself for life.

Relationships are fated; you can't just go find one that's going to automatically work. You can't *make* them happen. If you think about it you have to admit that of all the people in the world very few are really attractive to you. You turn down a lot of opportunities before someone happens along who really turns you on.

Love has an element of both surprise and surrender; there are no set rules, despite promises of the books that can list them for you chapter and verse. Our inner coding for partners is very subtle, and our feelings of attraction come out of the deep subconscious. Have you ever noticed how many people marry someone that looks like their parent? There is always an attraction to both the positive and negative attributes of your father and mother in a partner. I don't mean to suggest that relationships are the pot that boils out the dregs of your inner conflicts. It's simply that at this point in human history, relationships are in an evolutionary process that is still very confusing. Love stories are just that—stories. Real relationships have to be tested.

Society once dictated our relationship choices. It deemed that proper relationships be more oriented to the satisfaction of the male. Perhaps that is why over 50 percent of young people today who are polled on marriage say they don't want to get married. Now we are pioneering unexplored territory. Appropriate relationships in Western cultures certainly aren't dictated by society. Divorce isn't considered an unforgivable failure anymore. Now we're willing to do something unique—to join romantic love, sexual passion, and a commitment that is based on an equal footing in a single and lasting relationship. Or at least that's the goal.

Today we have our relationships on four areas of compatibility: mental, emotional, sexual, and spiritual. Exploring these areas with a partner takes time and considerable trial and error; to create a complete relationship we must develop a new level of intimacy, acknowledging and moving past the fear, anxiety, and distrust that continues to keep us apart emotionally.

Astrology is a source of information that will help you to understand the gifts of your love nature and how you react to commitment. It also reveals the challenges that keep you from the deep and lasting love you want.

Traditional astrology describes which signs are compatible and which aren't. Many good books have been written on this subject and I have learned from and appreciate them. However, it's time to go beyond the process of categorically labeling people to being able to interpret the information you're given by knowing a potential partner's Sun sign. Like being freed from the shackles of arranged marriages, soul-based astrology in this Aquarian age gives you the freedom to choose—but choose with a educated mind and an open heart.

By being attuned to your own spiritual consciousness, your soul, you have a better chance of knowing how to respond to your partners. This takes time and patience. We contact our soul and awaken our deeper nature through our emotions. Without the awareness of our feelings we cannot associate the effects of fear, sadness, anger, and joy with their causes. Sometimes, we don't even know which voice within us is speaking from the head, and which voice is speaking from the soul. Remember, head talk that comes from painful emotions is self-negating. The voice of the soul is always hopeful.

The soul may give you information you don't want to hear, but there is a feeling of openheartedness that energizes and activates your thoughts and actions. With this internal support you move past survival and security concerns into a new vision of love that will make your own life experience more joyful and will help shape a new world in the process. Your relationship becomes an unfolding process of discovery and revelation. A connection to *your very own soul* is a prerequisite for your peace of mind and essential to a healthy, fulfilling relationship.

To create an equality in a relationship that has a chance of real survival, you must look to the soul of your partner. When you are soul connected you can feel it: a sense of well-being floods your heart, a sweetness all its own.

As a practicing astrologer I find there are couples who are able to create rich and rewarding relationships without having traditionally compatible signs. They are willing to be soul connected. On the other hand I have seen people whose charts show that they are supposedly very compatible who don't stay married a year. Why? There are often deep-seated problems that their charts only hint at, and I've found that you have to live out a relationship for at least a year to know what the problems are. I'm not saying that the traditional aspects that we look for in compatibility charts are untrue; it can make the hard times easier to be with someone who has compatible responses to stressful situations.

There is no easy solution to allowing ourselves the vulnerability of love. When you choose a mate, you take on not only your own problems but theirs as well. Your partner's chart is superimposed on top of yours and their gifts and challenges become a part of your strengths and weaknesses. That's a sobering thought. If we surrender to the fact that love isn't easy, it gets easier. Our expectations change and we can create new intentions and actions that are more mature, and yes, more loving.

Apollo was the god of the Sun, and as the patron of Sun sign astrology he has much to teach us. He was a god of science, mathematics, and archery and also ruled the deeper awareness that lies beneath conscious mind. He was known as a reconciler of opposites, and his creed was everything in balance. The natal Sun sign in your chart is much like Apollo. It is the key to mental and emotional balance in your life. Each Sun sign by its very nature has positive and negative attributes and, even more important, the ability to reconcile these opposites.

I feel in this new age, we must move past the simplistic "We're both water signs" compatibilities into true soul connections. We can put the separated Platonic male and female partners, figuratively speaking, back together with deep love and compassion. You don't have to go outside yourself to find this state; it's there inside of you already, drawing your perfect partner like a magnet. When you attract someone who is willing to be your life mate, the sense of joining is like coming home.

Your partner reflects back your own character, your own inner nature, which makes life interesting and a challenge. Not only will you find areas of compatibility, but the parts of yourself that are incomplete or that you denied will be played out in your relationship. Of course, this can cause problems. You mustn't forget—*that which attracts, also repels.*

In a partnership, each person uses the other as a reference point to establish his or her own identity. Partnerships are in a constant process of change and a great deal of the interaction in a relationship is unconscious. The spirit of love is a mystery. It's enough to keep you on your toes your whole life. A soul-full relationship that grows in intimacy offers two of the greatest challenges: one is to know yourself and the other is to know the soul of your significant other.

Your Sun sign is coded the same way a seed in nature is predestined to be a certain kind of plant. There is a wonderful song in an off-Broadway show called *The Fantasticks*; it goes, "Plant a carrot, get a carrot, not a brussels sprout." The same goes for astrology. Astrology tells us our characteristics; what we do with that information is up to us. If you are a Leo, you are a Leo. You don't see the world like a Pisces. There can be affinity between these two signs, but a fire and water sign come from such a different perspective, they could spend more time explaining their position to each other than developing a relationship. Each would capture the other's imagination, yet the fire could burn the fish and the water could drown the lion. There would need to be a willingness on the part of both people to create a comfortable atmosphere that is conducive to intimacy and safety. It may seem impossible but it's not; relationships are about exploring compatabilities and conflicts.

No matter how much you love someone there are always things about the other person you don't like. These negative qualities are necessary: without an aspect of confrontation there is no attraction. With the information about yourself you glean from others, you can have more self-awareness. A shared experience can bring the greatest joy, and without the force of objectivity there is no consciousness, there is no life experience. The kind of relationship you create is up to you: your Sun signs, and your partner's, simply provide the material to explore the permutations and the possibilities.

Part I
Are You Compatible?

Love, Romance, and the Soul

The question I'm asked the most often is "Are we compatible?"

After one of my public appearances, a couple will furtively come up to me, and one spouse will say, "I'm a Scorpio and my partner is a Leo. Astrology books say our signs aren't harmonious; will our marriage last?" There is an urgency in their voices as if their "incompatible" Sun signs were time bombs. "Must we stand by and watch as our relationship self-destructs?"

Of all the people who come to me for astrological consultations, very few marry the sign with whom they are considered to be compatible. I feel that one of the main attributes of the Aquarian age is that you have the right to be an individual and complete within yourself, but what this does to relationships is still to be discovered. Most of my astrology readings are about relationships; not so much who you're compatible with, but how to have a working relationship with the one you're with already.

Even couples with traditionally compatible signs fear conflict and seem to be unsure of the securing of their relationship. With half of the marriages ending up in the divorce court you can understand their alarm, but I'm always a little surprised at their feelings of helplessness. Can it be that astrology is giving out the wrong message? The age of Pisces, whose influence is fading daily as we go deeper into this new century, was a time when organized religion controlled marriage. With two thousand years ahead of us in the age of Aquarius, astrology will evolve as an empirical source of information. In this new age we will develop a larger vision and be aware of the power and creativity that arise out of the play of differences.

Love Transcends Differences

Relationships are not only about togetherness.

You must learn to see that each day is a chance to experience your partner in a different way, and that the problems that naturally arise are full of possibilities for growth and change.

There is an old American Indian saying: "Take two birds and tie them together. You have two heads, four wings, and four feet, but they can't fly." After intense moments of connection you and your partner naturally retreat into separateness and feel yourselves as separate poles. This pause gives you the space to be who you are and stimulates the desire to come together again. And after all, aren't relationships the union of separate beings? We need a sense of our own space, our own identity, to be intimate.

In my astrology practice I've read many compatibility charts for couples. It has never occurred to me to tell couples with classically incompatible Sun signs to end their relationship; I give them insight on how to circumvent and transform the problems that arise. Basically incompatible signs such as Scorpio and Leo can develop a soul-bonded relationship, and even compatible signs generate a whole set of issues that have to be sorted out if a relationship is to succeed.

I find there are three basic types of relationships: one is to become involved with someone like yourself in world-view and emotional responses; another is to become involved with someone totally your opposite; then there are the *alien* relationships where you become involved with someone from a totally different background or culture and everything they do is fascinating or confusing. Romance has widened its territories so that today your partner logically could be from a different culture, race, and/or religion. These relationships have no chance of working without an understanding of how the process of love develops into intimacy.

Compatible or Not

Our greatest gift in life is choice.

It is important to remember that nothing in life is so ordained that it can't be changed. At every moment in time and space we have a 100 percent chance to make a decision through love or from a sense of need. Even if you and your partner have Sun signs that are traditionally incompatible, the soul inherently manages and transcends the influences of the stars.

There are couples who, according to their charts, aren't supposed to be compatible at all, who never have an argument, but even with the best of aspects there are no promises. To explain this you must understand what astrology offers you. Your Sun sign doesn't control you in any way. It's a subtle influence much like your nationality or the physical and emotional characteristics that you inherit from your family.

You can live your life very well without the benefit of astrology, but once you see how it influences your life it can become a valuable tool for self-help. The soul transcends time and space; it can use the energy of your Sun sign in several ways.

One of the obstacles to lasting marriages is that most mating is done in our twenties. Face it! Few of us are mature at that time. But even when people put off commitment until later there are no guarantees. Of course you have more life experience to draw from, but dating at any age is difficult because it requires vulnerability and risk. When I predicted a relationship for her, a single client of mine in her fifties moaned to me, "It's unnatural to date in your fifties."

Each stage of courtship and commitment brings new choices and a chance to grow closer. At each point we create a new path and a new life lesson. We have much more power to achieve what we want than we give ourselves credit for.

As we move into the new century, it is possible for people to live longer. There has to be respect, patience, and simple endurance, as well as love, to be married for fifty years or more.

Aquarian Age Relationships

Astrology doesn't have all the answers.

Astrology is a system we work through, much like a cosmic weather report. Astrology is a road map for spiritual growth and an invaluable source of information. There are two things in life that you can't change: that you are born into the earth plane and that eventually you will leave it. While you're here, you spend a lot of time trying to find out what life is all about, usually by interacting with others. In fact, the meaning of life is found primarily through relationships; that is the game of life. You have a choice in how you play the game, but to know yourself you must relate to others.

One day, there is a wake-up call: you lose your job; your partner asks for a divorce; someone dear to you dies; you may become seriously ill. Generally this call means that your life as you have known it is over. However it happens, suddenly your perspective changes and you need answers to questions you've never asked. Why am I here? Why did this happen to *me*? With new awareness and close scrutiny you find you possess undesired traits or handicaps as well as wonderful gifts or talents to use without much effort. This elevated conscious awareness looks past the obvious into the subtle. You can see the signature of the Creator.

Astrology is a great help; as a holistic tool for self-knowledge, it gives you pieces of the puzzle you wouldn't see otherwise. By observing your life as you live it, things you've overlooked in the past are more apparent. You find there are no coincidences, everything is connected, full of purpose and meaning. All of creation is one great unity and every minute counts. By putting the pieces together in a cohesive way you are able to help others see it too.

Aquarius is the sign of unity, and unity will be our lesson for the next two thousand years. When you learn that you are whole at a deep level of consciousness, then you won't expect outside things or other people to fill the emptiness inside or complete you. Then your relationships will improve, no matter what sign you are.

You can read every book, magazine, and newspaper in the world and still not understand what is really happening in your life and around you until you look within and come to the conclusion that life is a creative experience. When you take responsibility for the quality of your life, then you will be ready to attract and sustain a truly intimate and fulfilling relationship.

Soul-Centered Relationships

Astrology is a usable system and Aquarian astrology is a new way of looking at this ancient information.

Hidden in the zodiac's timeless symbols are potentials and possibilities. How you react to the compelling aspects of your

Sun sign is your choice. People have changed very little physically through the ages, yet the world is very different today.
We function today with a strong degree of personal autonomy, which would have been considered sacrilegious to the
ancient mind.

Spiritual principles have been lost by choosing an intellectual approach to life instead of a holistic view. The ancients
believed in a divine force through which the spiritual and
physical universe becomes manifest. Because their religion
and science was connected, they understood the force that
permeates and links all levels of reality from the divine to the
most material. Nature was an important part of their lives.
We have lost this understanding in the last century and our
world has been wounded by this separatism.

In the Aquarian age partnering can be done on an equal-
footed basis. Relationships aren't based on what I can do for
you or you can do for me, but what we can do together.

> *The Aquarian motto for relationships: I love you
> enough to give you the space to follow your own
> soul path and I want to share my life with you as
> you are.*

Love comes from the soul. The more secure you are within
yourself, the more soul connected you are and the better your
chances of having a lasting relationship. To be happy with
someone there must first be the vulnerability to join emotionally, mentally, sexually, and spiritually with another human
being. When you surrender to your soul, a great source of
wisdom is tapped. You move past the level of natural affini-
ties into mature understanding and the ability to weave yourself into another's life. You can see more possibilities and find
solutions, no matter what your differences.

The hope of success in marriage, or any relationship for
that matter, is to realize that the commitment is of itself an
opportunity for you to mature. With so much emphasis on

individuality in today's world we are so self-absorbed that there may be too much of an inclination to gratify ourselves, instead of understanding our partner's needs. Are you trying to make someone (anyone) love you without thinking objectively about the total picture? Are you using love as an aphrodisiac for your ego?

Secure within yourself, you can reach out to others without fear of loss. As you learn to accept yourself, you accept others. You must respect the simple everyday events of life as a way of building intimacy. You must let go of the feeling of the need to control the future. Wanting to make someone love you becomes redundant. The magic of love lies in the unknown. Love can't be controlled; it is a mystery and we are all seekers.

In Transition to a New Age

Astrology is ruled by Aquarius. The symbols of astrology coded with endless knowledge will move into power as a beacon for transformation. As we enter the Aquarian age the primary frontier will be how to handle truth and honesty. There will be no secrets. At this time the Piscean age, with its vision of self-expression as well as self-delusion, still prevails in our society. As we go through this transition from one age to another, we still have the conditioned responses of past history and traditions. Many of these have been fraudulently emotional and flagrantly dishonest.

As the Aquarian age of electricity and worldwide communications moves forward, you will have the chance to expand mentally and spiritually.

With so much information available, you *must* exercise your ultimate freedom—the ability to choose your attitude and actions in a given set of circumstances. Morally you have the power to choose what you want as long as it doesn't hurt anyone else. This calls for, as Victor Frankl says in his book *Man's Search for Meaning,* "taking on the responsibility of passing the torch to independent and inventive, innovative and creative spirits." The challenge will be how to sort out the superfluous, the trite, and know what is usable and valuable.

Aquarian age astrology is a wonderful help in such complex times. The point is not so much whether you are compatible with your mate or not, but what in your nature needs work to keep your intimacy bond intact. As we move forward in time, relationships will not be based on living up to other people's ideas of your responsibility, or the fear of God's wrath. It's simply a matter of creating a space of equanimity with your partner through trust and, yes, real love.

The Aquarian age will open the door to new dimensions of understanding. We are being forced to simplify our lifestyles and practice our values. At this time with the media ruthlessly grabbing news like swarms of sharks feeding on one piece of bait, we hear more than we ever wanted to hear on one subject. There will be no secrets. The truth will be there, but it is so fragmented that it takes a person who is psychological and spiritually developed to know what is real and what is not. In the past we didn't know the facts about the personal lives of people in power. Now we do, whether we want to or not. Nothing is hidden, but it can also be distorted. We must face the facts, but the truth is still just as elusive as it was before the information age. This is true in all aspects of our lives, in our places of business as well as in our homes.

A Path of Detachment

Astrology as a system is totally without attachment; you are neither good nor bad.

There is no psychological system that goes so impartially into the heart of the matter as quickly as astrology. In my first book *Soul Signs,* I explain that each sign is endowed with a unique gift—a person's Soul Power—and the aspect of a person's personality that can stand in the way of personal growth and development, their Ego Blockage. Your Soul Power and Ego Blockage relate directly to the gift and challenge of your Sun sign's approach to love. When you operate out of your Soul Power, you have the absolute confidence in yourself needed to open your heart, and your relationships are greatly improved. If you look for someone else to make you complete, you'll be very disappointed. Knowing your Ego Blockage can help you be aware when you are acting out of selfishness, not love.

We are really all alike in a spiritual sense. There is a divine spark that dwells in everyone. The reason you are alive is to connect with your own soul. Our purpose is to live a life filled with love. We are here to experience joy. The secret is to be at ease with yourself and to be in harmony with what is happening in your life, no matter how uncomfortable. This is a struggle we share with everyone. We are here at this time because we choose to go through this great transition together.

A Piece of Reality

Your horoscope tells you about your talents and your weaknesses.

Astrology is so applicable to the human condition that even your personal horoscopes in magazines and daily newspapers are amazingly accurate, especially if they are written by excellent astrologers. Your Sun sign describes a level of interconnectedness among the rest of your Sun sign family; yet you still act out the individual characteristics that originated on your own birth day, at your birth time, in your own way.

After using astrology for thirty years, I know that it opens you to parts of yourself very quickly and, even more important, these hidden parts of you can be revealed, retrieved, and integrated. By taking these attributes to heart, you leave behind a lot of confusion, become more conscious, and make better decisions. In his book *Pope's Sayings*, Alexander Pope said, "Know then thyself presume not God to scan, the perfect study of mankind is man." Study your Sun sign, your ascendant, and your Moon sign. Find out and read about your sweetheart's Sun sign as well. It helps to know the one you're with. Your sign is coded; you might even say it's fated with certain inner attributes that are entirely predictable.

Astrology Versus Science

Hard logic takes the heart out of astrology; it is an art and a science, but it can't be proved scientifically. Our present scientific method is an excellent system that collects isolated facts and carries through to a logical conclusion. This rational system, as great as it is for certain subjects, can't be used accurately in the subtle areas of life involving emotions and feelings, which can't be seen or measured.

Science is ruled by Aquarius, a fixed and stubborn air sign. There is much competition in the scientific field and there is a tendency to become rigid and fanatical—freezing out the ideas of the original theoretician. The inflexible scientific orientation of present-day thinking undermines a natural sense of spiritual balance in that it leaves out a lot of information. We need more emphasis on a holistic approach. Human problems are being neglected. Your inner nature can't be measured. You're not a statistic. Even if you go into your subconscious with a floodlight you can't see everything stored in there all at once. Your feelings can't be sorted out and categorized, even though you might try. Your Sun sign tells you what qualities you are working with, not what is going to happen or what you will do. Nothing is so drastic that you can't change your attitude about it or so good that all your problems are swept away. Remember your soul is always there giving you insight and courage to handle everything you picked to go through in this lifetime.

A Science in Itself

Sadly, in this age of so much information, we are all thrown into a jungle of possibilities without a firm guiding synthesis.

Alan Watts, in his book *Nature Man and Woman*, says, "Thought, with its serial, one-at-a-time way of looking at things, is ever looking to the future to solve problems which can be handled only in the present, but not in the fragmentary present of fixed and pointed attention."

In the world today it seems we are required to accept a mechanical reason for everything. Without the understanding of your unconscious you lose sight of the whole and become fragmented, mentally and emotionally. Astrology helps by giving meaning to life situations you couldn't see otherwise. It helps you to find solutions that otherwise would fall through the net.

You must realize that not everything that counts can be counted. An eternal lightness of being animates your human form. It is the soul that has humans, not the reverse.

The very essence of the soul is liberation. The word *psyche* means "soul." If you look it up in the dictionary, the original meaning for *psyche* is from the Greek word for "breathe." (It is interesting that so many of the words having to do with higher consciousness in different cultures come from words meaning "breath of God.")

Courtship and Commitment

The biggest surprise of all is that deeply coded in the evolving symbols of the zodiac are clues to positive steps of courtship and soul bonding.

The zodiac is a series of twelve phases that lends itself to the complex subject of falling in love and making a commitment. Starting from Aries, which rules the head, and going all the way around the zodiac to the feet or finalizing point in Pisces, you'll find a developmental flow that will help you to keep an account of where you are when you are in a relationship. By learning these phases you can stay balanced and go through key points where relationships get stuck, progress, or dissolve. These are guidelines only; instead of limiting you they support you in meeting your goal of true love.

"Come and play with me," proposed the little prince.

"I cannot play with you," the fox said. "I am not tamed."

"What does that mean—'tame'?"

"It is an act too often neglected," said the fox. "It means to establish ties."

"'To establish ties'?"

"Just that," said the fox. "To me, you are still nothing more than a little boy who is just like a hundred thousand other little boys. And I have no need of you. And you, on your part, have no need of me. To you, I'm nothing more than a fox like a hundred thousand other foxes. But if you tame me, then we shall need each other. To me, you will be unique in all the world. To you, I shall be unique in all the world. . . ."

—Antoine de Saint-Exupéry, *The Little Prince*

Part II
How the Twelve Signs of the Zodiac Correspond to the Twelve Phases of Every Relationship

Love Is Magic—or Is It?

Who can explain how or why people fall in love?

Thousands of songs, poems, and films have been made about the course of love. As long as we have hearts that throb with passion we will be fascinated and enamored with love's mystery.

I am asked about love more than any other subject. I used to think women were interested in love and men in business. Wrong! Men want to hear about their love life first; *then* it's business. Yes, a good astrologer can see possibilities of love and important timing in your chart; some times are better for romance than others, and some people are more compatible than others. But there is absolutely no guarantee that things will pan out the way you want or expect. These aspects of love are only windows of opportunities. The truth is, relationships are work. That doesn't sound romantic at all, does it?

When it comes to love at this time in history, we are all over the place, totally led by our feelings with no real idea of what we can realistically expect, if anything. There were times when families picked our mates for us; this is true in some countries even today, but now most people prefer independence and want to learn how to live freely and make their own selection—without anyone's approval. Few of us live in neighborhoods where societal structure influences our selections, or societies where we have picked out our mate by the time we leave for college. In the 1950s, when I was in college, if a young woman wasn't "pinned" (wearing someone's fraternity pin) before she graduated she had failed at college, no matter what her grade point average.

As an astrologer I am able to observe many people's lives, and I have come to the conclusion that to build a good and lasting relationship there are certain phases that must be gone through. Becoming a couple is a matter of predictable unfolding passages, and the zodiac can tell you a lot about your partner's life path. But it shows much more than that—it holds valuable information about the evolution of your relationship, and sheds reliable information on the natural development and the maintenance of that relationship, from beginning to end.

We mustn't forget that all of these stages are magic. There must be attraction, chemistry, and a decision to be together. Two people need to, in some miraculous way, come to the same decision, at pretty closely the same time.

Each sign of the zodiac defines a clear and precise phase of development with its own special emotional issue that needs to be resolved before you can proceed comfortably to the next phase from courtship through commitment.

This is not to say that you are controlled in any way. You can get married at stage four, which is the phase of exclusivity ruled by Cancer. This stage can easily be mistaken for true love, although it's really a going-steady type of phase. There are two more logical stages before marriage: stage five, Leo, the lovely "in love" stage; then stage six, Virgo, where everything that's wrong shows up and must be sorted out. This is the phase that must be traversed for a relationship to proceed with any hope of lasting. Many people end their relationship here, but if they are patient and work through this cycle the relationship becomes stronger.

Sometimes one partner gets stuck in a phase while the other goes forward. If you are aware of the different phases, you can see what's really happening, and that can help you stay the course until you and your lover are both in the same place.

The first sign of the zodiac, Aries, signifies a state of primal attraction. Awakened to new possibilities, we circle around the zodiac going through each relationship phase. Our final destination is Pisces. This phase contains the potential for soul bonding, which has been there as a possibility from the first moment. But as the old wives say, "Many is the slip between cup and lip." No matter how much you are interested, the Aries cycle likes to start things—not necessarily to finish them; but remember, your romantic destiny is in your hands.

> *"What I think & what I feel can be my inspiration but it is then also my pair of blinders. To see one must go beyond the imagination and for that one must stand absolutely still as though in the center of a leap."*
>
> —John Cage, *Silence*

Getting Ready for Love

*"To believe in Love is to know that all your stars
are lucky ones."*

—Diane Eichenbaum, *Soul Signs in Love*

Self-Acceptance

The key to opening the door to a great source of understanding is to simply accept responsibility for how your life is turning out.

You may not be in control of a lot of things here on earth but you can work on the most important relationship you have: the one you have with yourself. The key to creating a loving relationship is total self-acceptance.

Our heavenly soul is ancient and timeless while our earthly body is new, a part of nature and the world. No matter how evolved you become mentally, how much information you pour into your brain, your true nature comes from this intermingling of body, mind, and soul. The result of this joining is that there is a part of your consciousness that is totally loving and supportive at all times. If you trust it, you become more secure in yourself.

The Hawaiian kahunas call this loving, detached part of us the *Amakua*. They say it is the highest of three separate and totally different selves that are components to our being-ness. The first is the basic self, the second is the mind, and the third, the *Amakua,* is a totally balanced male and female essence. This is the aspect of your soul that loves and supports you throughout life, totally there for you in every way. It is utterly reliable and constantly on call.

Trusting this part of yourself creates a self-acceptance that stands as the constant background of every thought, feeling, and action—however restricted physically or emotionally you might feel. To accommodate this underlying sense of integrity, sincerity, and peace of heart, you must embrace yourself. Then your sense of comfort and safety endures beneath every disturbance.

To be in this exceptional condition, you must make an inward commitment to yourself to be just who you are. This entails feeling exactly what you feel at every moment. This acceptance is not about excusing yourself lightly or indulging your moods, it's a recognition of where you really are coming from and taking the chance to grow. A feeling of safety comes from knowing you are blessed to be yourself and actually encouraged by your soul power to express your feelings and share your life with others.

The solution to any problem has to be learned in the problem itself and not away from it. Accusations and complaints are feelings that need to be expressed. Too many people sit on the fence, waiting for their significant other to wake up to their needs. After you accept your feelings as a necessary expression to intimacy, the next step is trusting that resolution is possible.

If you believe in resolution it's not the bitter end every time you have a disagreement.

Remember each Sun sign has its own special challenge. For instance, an Aries wants to confront the problem and fix it. A Libra will disengage and be silent; they hate confrontation. But these two signs are always attracted to each other. It's important to know your partner's pattern. What are his gifts? What are his challenges? What stage of relationship are you in? What can you expect next? That's what this book is about.

One of the most important aspects of building a good relationship is learning how to be in touch with your own emotions and how to share them with your partner. No matter how compatible you are, there will be conflicts. The ability to express your thoughts and feelings is a treasured mark of your maturity. But how do you create a neutral environment? It takes time. A relationship can't be hurried. There is a point in a courtship when you know that you can trust your partner. Congratulations! You have entered a phase when you have developed the good communication needed to heal the conflicts that inevitably come up. The pain of hurt and disappointment that always comes up in a relationship doesn't have to be swept under the rug. Each test opens you to new levels of understanding. After each trial there is a chance to create a closer bond.

There is a time in all lasting relationships when you know your partner inside and out. You love and trust this person with all your heart. Then you know that the process of developing a solid relationship, although it may have been painful at times, was worth it. You will feel like your other half, your long lost soul mate, is back in place—back home where he or she belongs.

Questions to Ask Yourself in Preparation for a Committed Relationship

1. Do you feel you have a good relationship with yourself?

2. Are you truly willing to open your time to someone else?

3. Are you willing to risk and realize you have no control over the outcome?

4. Everyone needs to be safe, to be healed, and to feel whole. Do you know your own individual inner needs in a relationship?

5. Are you ready to open your heart and your emotional needs to someone else?

The Twelve Phases of a Relationship

*"Love one another, but make not a bond of love:
Let it rather be a moving sea between the shores of
your souls."*

—Kahlil Gibran, *The Prophet*

Courtship

Aries—Phase 1: Being Interested

*The beginning of love holds the potential for the magic of
Eros. Life's full pulsation is there in one person. You are interested in pursuing this delight and plunge headfirst and
fearlessly into change.*

In Pursuit of Love

In the beginning God created the heavens and the earth.
"Let there be light," it says in the first chapter of Genesis, and
the world as we know it was born. Aries rules this act of genesis—of birth—and the core essence of this self-motivated
sign is love.

As the first sign in the zodiac, Aries starts the whole cycle of relationships. It rules the moment there is the first possibility of love. Spontaneous and eager, Aries energy is expressive of the beginning of a relationship. This is when someone catches your eye and you say, "Hi!"

Aries rules the feelings that are necessary to create bonded relationships. This stage is about more than just checking out the territory, but we do have the right to have a wish list and to check off more than half of the major points for the fit to be right. What's on the list is your choice, but I suggest you start the list with these three things. You can get as specific as you want.

People You Want to Date

1. People who can meet you halfway with open hearts.

2. People who earn your trust and have proven their loyalty.

3. People who are willing to take the time to get to know you better.

This list is made up of characteristics that can't support a relationship.

People You Must Not Date

1. Anyone who is not available, *whatever* the cause.

2. Anyone who is actively abusing themselves with substances such as drugs or alcohol.

3. Anyone who abuses you emotionally and/or mentally.

Perhaps you need to have a few dates before you understand the situation, but when you know—that's that. You might think that everyone comprehends these things, but many people call me devastated about their loved one's behavior, and yet they knew it from the beginning. They just didn't think it would hurt *them*.

It takes real guts to enter into a relationship. The beginning of a relationship is so much fun, with your feelings so stimulated, that it's easy to forget about the risk of being hurt and recklessly jump in. Meeting someone new is romantic and infinitely entertaining. What do you have to lose? There is a sense of "anything's possible" that makes you feel quite giddy. You are fearless with hope and you don't have much emotion invested at this point. Yet this mutual vulnerability is one of the greatest gifts of love. We must learn to love that part of our soul that isn't rational, that seeks love, even when it may seem foolish to others. Nothing ventured nothing gained, right? So get out and mingle.

Taurus—Phase 2: The Seduction

This is the stage where you click. The chemistry starts. You find yourself thinking about your potential partner with desire and want to see this person again. There is a sense of expectancy that is very enticing and gets the adrenaline kicking.

All You Need Is Love

Venus rules Taurus and there is a feminine and magnetic principle at work here. This phase may begin on the first date or after several months of dating. I have a client who worked side by side with her future husband for five years and they never even noticed each other. One day, no different than any other day, he asked her to join him on a coffee break. From that moment on they were together. Chemistry isn't always an explosion; it can sneak up on you. Many times it comes when you least expect it—your logic goes out the window and you feel a whirl of passion that opens up a feeling of ecstasy.

When ecstasy is evoked you are able to stand outside of yourself. You are filled with an emotion so powerful that you are transported to another realm. In daily life we rarely step outside of ourselves. We have to work, make decisions, we are constantly thinking, planning, and doing. It is one of the gifts of God and nature that we have the ability to experience attraction so uplifting that we are transported to a place that is timeless, spaceless, where we can experience the flow of life at its highest level. It makes life worth living.

It's no wonder that we want to stay in this exciting dimension as much as we can. Since it can be artificially stimulated, the senses are easily fooled. This is why at an early stage like this, even though you may want to step outside of logic, having a code of dating that protects you is a good thing. The old "no sex on the first date" has given many a person a chance to stop behavior that would be regretted the next day. But, however you handle the flow of mutual receptivity, of knowing that there is chemistry at work, it is still a gift of life to know the vibes are right for a good relationship. Just remember there's no hurry. By honoring the awareness of the attraction but putting off sexual intimacy until you are comfortable with the logistics, you are taking good care of yourself.

Many people confuse the feeling of sexual attraction for intimacy and real love. It isn't. That's why you need a space of time to check out the situation and find out if you are projecting your feelings off onto your partner. When hormones are raging it's easy to assume he or she is thinking like you. The truth is, at an early stage of dating you would be assuming a lot to think that way. Then of course in the world today, where sex is honored without the gift of love, it's still your decision, but sex for recreation has a price that is emotionally expensive to pay.

Although this is a phase of courtship where physical attraction is important, it is not the only process going on. We all operate on many subtle dimensions. Your feeling of wanting to passionately come together is just one level of bonding. This stage is more than just sex. You may have a feeling of peace and joy just holding hands. This is a more soulful connection with a feeling of completeness that doesn't need anything else. When you are enclosed in this wonderful sense of euphoria your trust level increases and you find yourself able to share with this person in a way that's very edifying.

What's important to remember is that this is not a phase of commitment, you're only testing the water. In this transitional stage you still might be going out with others. But if there is chemistry it has a chance of growing into a full relationship.

Gemini—Phase 3: Pursuit

This is a dating phase. By going out and having a good time, meeting your partner's friends and family, you find out if there is enough compatibility to take the relationship further. You can still date others but this relationship is a good thing and you know it.

Love Talk

You've met someone you're interested in and have had a few dates. Long ago there was still a chaperon at this phase to ensure proper behavior. Gentlemen came to call. Everyone dressed up in their best and sat down for tea and had a social conversation. How things have changed! No one wants that kind of limitation in their socializing these days. However, I have noticed that young people date in groups now, so maybe it's not so different as you might think. Just talking about mundane things can bring a sense of familiarity at early stages of courtship. This important stage is about learning more about your partner, getting to know each other better. It's a time of watching him act and interact within a social group. Also a time of talking, talking, and more talking. The

Internet has become a tool many people use for this stage. But it's only the beginning.

Relationships take time to grow, but if your partner always wants to be alone, it could be a signal that there are some serious problems. It's important to look for a history of stability and dependability. Check the person out and see if he is responsible in his behavior. My mother always said, "It's not what they say, it's what they do that counts."

Look for honesty. It's better for the object of your affection to say, "I don't know if I'm ready for a serious commitment," because it means he's been thinking about what that entails. People who are the most eager to get heavily involved too soon are often living in fantasies of love. When the fantasy fades and the excitement is gone, often they are too.

Dating today often includes drinking and sometimes the offer of drugs. As you start being honest with yourself, you won't need such extreme means of escape to feel excited. In fact, that is a sure way to lose your inhibitions too soon and end up sorry. Honest, intimate communication has to be sober communication. An "exciting" relationship with someone unpredictable and volatile isn't a good choice. This kind of person won't be sensitive to your needs; they're too concerned with their own. The better partner is someone who respects your needs and who is open to learning something about you.

When you feel from the start that you need to help the person to whom you're attracted, be careful. Caretaking overly sensitive people with out-of-control lives isn't what you're looking for in an Aquarian age partnership unless you're looking for a road map for disaster.

This is a period of courtship where memories are made. "Remember the time when we made sandwiches and went sailing and saw that beautiful sunset?" "I remember at the dance that I saw you waiting for me and I knew that I was glad to be there, with you."

At this stage you still could be dating others, although it is becoming increasing clear that you have found someone that has the qualities that you want.

Cancer—Phase 4: Exclusivity

You are going steady and opening up emotionally to each other. You know that you are ready to become deeply involved and not date anyone else. This is a phase of building trust.

Building an Emotional Love Nest

The goal of dating is to eventually make a commitment. Now you're getting closer to your goal. You have gone through the first three stages and, wonder of wonders, it's working. You are having a great time together. You have been able to sort out the differences so far and you're ready to be exclusive.

Even if you haven't dated anyone else since the beginning, this stage is different. You are talking about your feelings and making plans for the future. This is a time when you're comfortable with the relationship as it is and you're willing to open new avenues of intimacy. You're sure in your heart of hearts that there is hope of creating a sound and lasting relationship.

Many people think that being exclusive is a final destination. It's not. This is the time when you are seen as a couple. People start to expect to see you together. When you show up alone everyone wants to know where your *significant other* is. You talk on the phone every day (or e-mail) and share your life with each other.

Many couples move in with each other at this phase. I feel this is a mistake; it puts too much pressure on the relationship. You are still getting to know each other and there can be some unhappy surprises. Being together all the time at this point doesn't give either partner space to get off by him- or herself and sort things out.

We all long for closeness and attachment, and yet at the same time we feel a deep need to be separate, to be alone and free. Some people are never comfortable with a commitment on any level, and some people will make a commitment just to be with someone. It's important not to be too serious at this time, to let the relationship sort itself out: if you want too much intimacy at the beginning it puts pressure on the relationship; if you need too much autonomy your partner's feelings often get hurt. Through good communication you are able to make the compromises necessary to grow together. There is a lot of work involved in this phase.

No relationship stays in harmony very long anyway; even the best of romances have their unstable moments. With two people involved there are always opposing viewpoints that are never totally resolved. Relationships are based on tension: without the stress there would *be* no relationship.

Your partner's differences create an attraction on one hand and force issues on the other. What seems magical and full of joy is right next to misunderstanding and confusion. This is based on the law of the universe that holds that opposites attract and repel at the same time.

The closeness being developed at this stage is still fragile. With a decision to be serious, there is also ambivalence that must be faced in order to move to the next level.

In a sane and mature courtship what happens is that you detach from the outcome and let it happen.

Leo—Phase 5: Falling in Love

Your heart beats wildly and your legs get weak. You realize it's love and it's mutual! This phase is pure enjoyment and your life takes on new meaning.

Love's Drama

I ask you, what is more wonderful than being in love? When two hearts beat as one, it's a feeling that can't be duplicated. Some people spend their whole life waiting for this magic moment. Nine times out of ten magically it does.

I have been reading charts for thirty years and I have predicted a lot of husbands. I can describe their looks and even what they do. These predictions are based on the aspects for a relationship found in the natal chart. Periodically there are windows of opportunity that are open to the possibility of love. Patience is required; sometimes you have to wait for the good aspects to fall in place. If your life isn't conducive to a healthy relationship when that window forms, there is always another time in the future.

Many people mourn their loneliness and feel they'll never meet anyone when that couldn't be further from the truth. It *is* hard if you're not getting any feedback. So get a life; learn something new. The important thing to do is to set up your life in a flexible way so that you encourage new people to be around you. If the window is open someone might just step through.

The best course is to enjoy this period of your life and keep growing. Take this time for yourself to do the things you may not be able to do later. The most important thing to do is to keep your heart open and set up your life so that a relationship is feasible. Sometimes in such busy times as we have now, that alone takes years to set up. The good news is that at this period of history men and women alike aren't being pushed into marriage by a certain age. Your heart is ageless and can always find someone to be with if you're open to new possibilities and are not trying to be in control.

This Leo stage of love at its best is a phase of mutual discovery and sharing. Some people think they're in love when it's really the adventure and joy of the events around them that are sustaining the relationship, rather than the mutual sharing. Intimacy grows through the nourishing experiences you share together—not the exciting events you're living. One couple I know thought they were madly in love when it was the political campaign they were working on they were in love with. Their relationship fizzled very fast after the election was over. That was the end of that. When it happens too quickly it's good to back off for a while and see if you're only in love with the excitement of love.

Virgo—Phase 6: Making a Decision

A crucial time of examining your relationship. It's wise to remember that this is a period that can create an unconditional love. Yet this is when many relationships fall on the floor.

Little Things Mean a Lot

After the initial excitement of wooing you move past the idealistic period into a serious stage where real decisions about a relationship's future need to be made. You can see things about your lover now that were not apparent earlier. Bothersome little things start coming up that catch your attention.

The concern you feel is natural to the process. Are the differences between you too extreme? Do you want to go on? I'm not talking about the obvious problems that were sorted out earlier. Everyone has a list of personal needs that have to be met and it doesn't take long to see if these are there. Now is when the anxiety of ambivalence kicks in and you feel a sense of displacement; wanting to go forward but still fearing loss of your freedom, you become confused and immobilized.

This is often a time of withdrawal. It's your right to choose what's best for you and you must allow for this period of vacillation. This is a crucial step and must be experienced to make a good decision. I think the major fear at this stage is, "If I love you, you will see my obvious faults and reject me."

You were having such a good time, then the evaluating and criticizing begins. "Why do you always leave the dishes in the sink when the dishwasher is right there?" You notice things like his suit is always rumpled or she doesn't empty her cat's litter box often enough. I once broke off with someone because his socks were the wrong color. I was so unaware of my real inner needs at that time that to look for the *real* problems was over my head.

This stage is created out of several different perspectives. One is that you are afraid of commitment. Another is that the more you know someone the more you know her frailties. What seemed charming at first is now getting on your nerves. Either way this is the turning point in a relationship and it is necessary to go through it if the relationship is to grow. Sometimes the love between you is so strong that you pass right by this difficult passage and never look back.

Out of nowhere it seems, the partner who was hot and heavy last week backs off. With changing sexual roles the female may have been the aggressive pursuer and then *she* doesn't call. Traditionally men move in and out of relationships while women continue to move forward and only back off when something upsets them. Perhaps men are slower to process their feelings, and emotions make them feel out of control. They need to retreat for a while to clear their heads. But this can be the same with women as well. Fear of real intimacy or being trapped kills a lot of budding courtships. Just remember that this is a normal occurrence and give your partner and the relationship some time.

The fear of losing yourself affects both sexes and brings a need for a break, but doesn't call for a disappearing act or a lame excuse; miscommunication can upset an otherwise very good match. Rejection is the hardest fact any person ever has to face in life; separation can't be handled too abruptly or the relationship is ruined. You must surrender your preconceptions. If this phase is circumvented by controlling behavior or denial, your relationship will be based on lies and is doomed to fail.

Once you both have made the choice to grow together, your view of the reality of your relationship changes. This new vision of love comes from a decision to be the creative force in your own life, not out of need, or out of conflict, but because it is what you want and you are committed to giving this relationship a chance. After you have gone through this phase and are out on the other side, you are more able to be involved with all of life, the bad times as well as the good.

Commitment

Libra—Phase 7: Marriage

This is the phase of knowing "this is it." You not only love this person but you're ready to make it permanent.

Buying the Ring

Romance and love are what everyone seeks. Yet it isn't as easy as you would think, people being like they are. Perhaps the true state of marriage, which symbolizes the inner marriage of opposites, is too subtle for us earthlings. Because of the high risk factor in romance there's nothing that teaches us more about ourselves than the pursuit of love. Still in every relationship there comes a day when you know at a deep level that you are ready to make plans for the future.

The *scale*, which is Libra's astrological symbol, illustrates this exactly. In the middle of the stress of opposites, at a point of perfect balance, a new energy is formed. This point of perfect tension is soulful understanding. This is where two hearts are poised, beating as one. This is a level where an enduring union is forged.

Cooperation and agreement are the most wonderful parts of a relationship. You've moved past vacillation—you're really getting somewhere. You've gone through the six courtship phases that lead to commitment; this usually takes about a year. You both know that this is it and you are *a couple on the verge*.

Phases of Courtship

1. You are interested.

2. You are attracted physically.

3. You have met each other's friends and family.

4. You are dating exclusively.

5. You've both proclaimed your love for each other.

6. You've gone through the hard part of backing off and checking out the difficulties of continuing the relationship.

Now is the time when you add accountability to your relationship, as you now see yourself as a committed couple. There are questions you must ask yourself at this stage, and you need to be honest with yourself and your partner. What are your expectations of marriage? How do you create the kind of intimacy that is comfortable to you both? By this time you know what your major areas of difference are, so are you willing to put something together that is permanent? Give yourself time until you can finally say:

- We love and respect each other.

- Let's make real plans to be together.

- Let's stand up and tell the world about our decision to make a commitment.

I suggest that you have at least a year of dating before making a commitment. I personally prefer two years; Mars, the planet of activation, takes two years to circumvent a chart. After every hard aspect in your chart has been set off, you both know how your significant other reacts under every type of situation. Going through crisis breaks down the false boundaries that we all hide behind. There is great joy and ecstasy from breaking down the walls of separation—and there's also pure agony. After learning to discriminate between constructive and destructive communication, you have the understanding needed to create something wonderful and enduring.

The committment to a lasting relationship does not have to include marriage. The difference there is that the announcement is left out. I personally think that to bring a courtship to fruition a marriage, secular or religious, is important. When you stand up in a ceremony before the world and announce your love, you enter into a sacred contract. All the love in the world blesses this union. That is why marriage is honored and is considered a sacrament in many religions. To be married with God's blessing is what Libra cherishes most. Remember that God is within your own heart. This perfect marriage of mind and feeling, heart and soul, is symbolized by the scales in balance. As human beings we strive to open to this great message of divine love in marriage.

At this point, the things that seem impossible to put up with are fading; so he is a little rumpled, he looks kind of cute and shabby chic is in. This stage of partnering brings a big sigh of relief as you know that you are truly loved and there is real hope for a future together. As different as you are, you love each other and you are willing to move forward and build a life together. The purpose of courtship up to this point has been to give you a chance to grow into a couple and to build an intimacy that is yours alone. Now you have something solid.

Scorpio—Phase 8: Creating Real Intimacy

Intimacy has been forming from the beginning, but this is the phase when you know you are connecting at a deep emotional level.

Passion at Its Highest

The cycle of courtship ends at Libra and now the phases of commitment come into play. The Scorpio phase is where the real bonding comes into the relationship: you commence the great adventure of living together. Now you have the joy of joining your lives together with love and respect. This is when your trust level is high and love develops into real intimacy. You both realize that you are in an equal partnership.

There is a line in the traditional marriage ceremony that says, "What God hath put together let no man put asunder." Inasmuch as your relationship is bonded at this point, no one *can* come between you. Libra, the first of the last six signs of partnership, rules the legal commitment and Scorpio rules the consummation and the benefits of a partnership.

It is interesting that Scorpio, the sign that rules sex and intimacy, comes *after* Libra, the sign of commitment and marriage. Perhaps the zodiac is telling us something. If there is sex before commitment, it is in the playtime of courtship; it does not have the depth of real feeling that comes after trust is shared later in the relationship.

Now you realize that you will share everything together. There is a whole new field of existence before you. What is left of the feeling of separateness slowly drifts away as everything becomes *ours* and *us*. This stronger bond is forged when you are able to love what is so, not just what you hope is so. When two people come together with open hearts the universe supports the union. Although there is great vulnerability, it is a satisfying phase—it's sustaining and healing to know that your partner has revealed himself to you in every way.

When two people share a sexual experience, the vital fire of the *kundalini shakti* is activated. Starting from the base of the spine, the vital energy goes from the genital area (body) up through the heart (soul) and into the head (mind). With a whirl of ecstasy, you are both unified in the perfect balance of the male and female bond. The rise of this great spiritual force causes a transformation of consciousness.

The true purpose of this phase is to ignite the tremendous power that is dormant in us all. Out of Egypt from the Thrice Great Thoth (later called Hermes in Greece) came the adage, "As above so below." The sign of Scorpio manifests this wisdom by opening the door to the subconscious, and in this phase of commitment you are invited to participate in actions so profound that you are changed at a cellular level. As physical as making love is, it is also deeply symbolic of the balancing of your body and soul. The love between two people can provide powerful glimpses of sacred vision. You have the ability to experience the most profound love experiences possible and you are the happiest and most fulfilled with one partner with whom you can combine emotional and sexual love.

The real purpose of sexual union is a beautiful surrender, a chance to share yourself completely with another. The centering that occurs aligns your body with your spirit. When your heart is opened by the flow of the kundalini energy, the barrier of ego breaks down and the mind clears, allowing creative energy to flow through. There is an exchange of energy that is uplifting and healing—the kind that makes life worth living.

In the world today the decision to have sex is often made very early in the courtship, sometimes *so* soon that it actually keeps the relationship from bonding. Although sex is a form of communication, when you are cut off from your feelings it can only serve as an intense physical and emotional exercise.

There is only a physical connection, not a deeper soul experience.

Since World War II there has been a tendency to rebel against society by having sex before marriage and often not even getting married at all. The benefits from marriage aren't considered important. This is a natural process of breaking down confining Victorian rules that were still prevailing until that time. But then problems started surfacing—children born out of wedlock, misuse of sex, child mothers, the abortion issue, and the spread of sexual diseases. The fear of diseases is joined with a more conscious state of being responsible for your actions.

Sexual relationships without a commitment of some kind may fall short of the real feeling of gratification. You can be in a sexual relationship for years and never achieve perfect sexual bonding. You have a better chance of achieving this liberating experience with communication, patience, and time. The thrill of a one-night stand dulls in comparison with the real intimacy shared by two people who have communicated both their needs and their vulnerabilities. Sharing life together with all of its disruptions and contradictions contributes to the depth and richness of your relationship.

Sagittarius—Phase 9: Setting Boundaries

Personal boundaries can be worked out easily after a state of trust has been set up. Every relationship is made up of two people who need space to be themselves. Then they have something to share.

Going the Distance

As you're busy gathering experiences, you must keep in mind that making a commitment brings in another person with his own independent ideas, and both of you have made a commitment to share your freedom with each other.

Sagittarius, the ruler of the third phase of commitment, sets the stage for personal freedom within a relationship. Scorpio may rule the phase of setting boundaries of intimacy, yet right next to that physical bonding process is Sagittarius, a sign of opening doors. It is a sign that allows for differences, and separation, and yet remains responsive. It is the nature of flexible Sagittarius to bend over backward to adapt to the situation.

Sagittarius rules openness. This is the time in a committed relationship where you are intimate with each other and you're not afraid to be honest. This kind of trust is built gradually, it is earned even under the best circumstances. When you reach this phase there is a sense of relaxation that gives the relationship a breather. This is when the ground rules of your relationship are laid. Such demands that are important to you are laid out and negotiated so that you can have a life of your own within your relationship. Even small accommodations like "I want to play golf every Saturday," "I can only cook three meals a week and do what else I have to do," are important.

Relationships are so individual to each couple that some couples even live in separate cities and keep a deep and sustaining intimacy alive. Another couple may be glued at the hip. We live at a time where there are few guidelines on this subject. It's often trial and error anyway, but that's the fun of it. Stretch yourself into a creative relationship. (Of course some of these borders change after children are born!)

If you've gone through the other phases of commitment and feel connected and safe, boundaries are easy to set.

Every couple is different. Because some people are afraid to ask for what they need and want, this phase is often delayed. You may wait until you are more comfortable in the relationship before you fess up to hating ball games even though you've been going with him for years.

Women and men have been programmed to hide their likes and dislikes for centuries. Men sometimes take it for granted that their wives will do whatever they do. Women often have a whole set of expectations usually based on the model of their own parents' commitment. These things need to be discussed and negotiated from a loving center just for you and your partner.

We always need to compromise in relationships. Slowly and surely each couple finds its way into a comfort zone that works and is mutually sustaining. Isn't it wonderful to have a loved one you can be with without talking for hours? Just knowing that you're connected in such a way is one of life's treasures.

The Sagittarian phase of love is unconditional and friendly. You can just love each other without an expectation. What a relief!

Capricorn—Phase 10: Achieving Goals

This is a decisive time in creating a solid relationship. It is a time of building something permanent, when there is a big outlay of time and money.

Let's Build Something Solid

Every couple has a different way of going forward on a pattern of soul bonding. When you are in the tenth phase of Capricorn, the cycle of commitment, you truly know that you can sustain—emotionally, mentally, and physically—a concrete future together. Even if this phase occurs during an engagement, with the wedding date set a year ahead, it shows that the courtship is going forward without any hitches.

In the twelve stages of relationships, Cancer, Libra, and Capricorn are signs of stabilizing decisions. Commitment could be made or a marriage take place in any one of these phases.

In the Capricorn phase, setting long-term goals together

makes a strong statement; it helps to hold people together in a tangible way. It can simply be buying a house or some other joint financial outlay, or it may be knowing that your relationship has moved to a deeper level emotionally. The phases of commitment are about much more than just romantic love: the commitment phases have to do with trust as well. One of the biggest ways of showing love and trust is to share space, time, and money on the physical plane. Promises that have been made earlier must be kept. Until you reach this phase of commitment there is a feeling of not knowing how to ground your relationship in the real world.

Capricorn is the sign that rules business. In the world today there are many decisions that need to made together. When couples don't go through this phase, these issues may come up when other forces come into play. For instance, if one partner makes all the financial decisions leaving one partner unaware of where they are financially, this dependence can cause damage to the relationship.

Not everything is decided on your wedding day. There are many surprises in store that help bring a couple together. Years later you can look back and see what you've built together financially and emotionally. No matter how much you love each other the marriage has to be created together. When you go through each phase of building a soul-bonded relationship you have something that you can rely on—something that is more precious than money. This process is really a course of maturation. Maturity isn't a box, it is the freedom to express yourself in the most evolved way and share your life with others. You can accept the limits a relationship entails, create trust in your partner, and allow freedom in your marriage. This takes a person who is willing to see things the way they are, not the way she would like them to be. The business end of marriage brings a sense of well-being that is priceless. When two people work together there is no telling how successful they can be. The sky's the limit.

Aquarius—Phase 11: Becoming Friends

A phase that slowly establishes the structure of relationships within and outside of a commitment. A phase of negotiation about who and what is important to both of you.

In Love We Are Created Equal

The phase ruled by Aquarius changes the borders of your outside relationships. When you are an established couple, you have built up a synergy that is an entity in and of itself. At the beginning of your relationship your friends are confronted with a decision on whether to accept your new partner into their lives. It can be a touchy subject. Because people are generally taught to be polite about such things usually no one says anything, but it doesn't take long for you to know when there is acceptance, distrust, or even out and out dislike. Sometimes we allow unhealthy situations to hang on in our lives until we meet someone. At that point our perspective is so changed that it doesn't bother us to move on into newer and better pastures.

Making the adjustments necessary to sustain your circle of friends is usually done as the dating process unfolds. The biggest part of this adjustment is inside your family unit. Families really do marry each other. Sometimes this is easy and sometimes it's not. If you've always had Sunday dinner with your folks, this is something that has to be settled with your partner. Maybe he will love the situation, maybe he will hate it. It's something that has to be worked out, and with respect and love it can.

The old adage, "Birds of a feather flock together," is based on a profound and hidden truth that we call synchronicity. This word, used by the great psychologist Carl Gustav Jung at the beginning of the twentieth century, can be translated as "meaningful coincidences."

Aquarius is the sign that rules this phenomenon. This relationship phase can be understood better when you know how to decipher the signs and clues within daily events that give you guidance. You have to allow yourself to be tuned to the subtlest energies. When you are committed to your partner and you've gone through all the stages of courtship and commitment together, it is then that you can trust the universe to guide you as a couple. You are always at the right place at the right moment no matter how difficult it may be for you to believe. Learning how to move into this subtle understanding is the big challenge of this phase. When you are in a deeply connected relationship it attracts like-minded others to be around you.

Sometimes there are a lot of extended family members to deal with—former spouses, children, even past lovers. This phase challenges your love and patience for each other as you work out the boundaries of these other relationships. Learning to negotiate with patience and honesty is particularly important at this time.

At the same time new friends and social situations are being attracted to the dynamic you've created together. It is possible for the old friends and the new ones to come together, but don't think you can control the outcome. You can only decide what your relationship is going to be in the world.

Pisces—Phase 12: Soul Bonding

There comes a day in your commitment that you are mentally, emotionally, physically, and spiritually bonded—connected by a love so profound that you are tied together by your very heart strings.

I Love You the Most

Pisces is a sign of unconditional love. This is the phase that brings heartfelt peace to both partners. Oddly some people tell me that from the very beginning they could feel the soul bond. They felt they already knew each other at a soul level and it helped them through many bad times. This doesn't happen in every relationship; in fact, I think that it is really a very rare experience. Most of the time we have to stumble through all the phases to build a relationship. This is really a reward stage. You have done the work and you're still together with hearts beating as one. It may take years for this phase to occur but it's always there waiting for you if you can learn how to love and trust each other.

Marriage is a spiritual path, but it is not necessarily an exalted path. Creating a more conscious commitment is a day-to-day struggle. There are no perfect people. We are all wounded to some degree. Being with someone in a commitment is really a decision to see your partner as he really is—a wounded child seeking salvation. From day one, after the fantasy part of the romance is over (and it *always* comes) you no longer assume that you can read your lover's mind. You learn to really listen to what is said and know that even if you don't agree your partner has the right to say it.

To accommodate the healing that is needed to salve the wounds of your earlier life, you must create an atmosphere that is safe and nurturing. If your partner has something to say that is critical of you, you can finally learn to know that this information can open doors for you. You are able to trust your partner's honesty and allow it to light up the dark corners of your soul where you have always been afraid to look. No one knows you better. As you both share your truth with each other you both reclaim parts of yourself that were lost. Slowly but surely, the unconscious fears, angers, childish ways, the old pain are brought to the surface to find acceptance and resolution.

When I say this is a peaceful phase—I don't mean that it isn't challenging. Our lives change constantly. We move up in our careers or down; we raise children, then they leave; the whole life process of aging is never boring. We are always forced to see things with new eyes. The peace I'm talking about is deep within you. Peace can even come from just being free to feel your negative emotions and express them. The key is that you need to feel safe to express yourself as you really are and know that you are loved. A peaceful marriage is a journey, not a destination. And it gets easier. You are lovers and you are passionate friends. Your love is infused with consciousness and will. You are kind, considerate, and honest because you have grown into a full understanding of how to be with the one you love. Then this peace goes out to others.

Part III
Soul Signs in Love

"And think not that you can direct the course of love, for love, if it finds you worthy, directs your course."

—Kahlil Gibran, *The Prophet*

Emotions Running High

"*Ever has it been that love knows not its own depth until the hour of separation.*"
—Kahlil Gibran, *The Prophet*

It is amazing how we delude ourselves. We seem totally incapable of seeing how much of our personal tragedy originates in ourselves, and how we continually feed it, keeping it going with a great loss of energy. All of us have areas of inner conflict—alienated parts of our personality which we want to deny. In fact, you can stay on the defensive until there is a wake-up call—a point in your maturation cycle that gives you the courage to look at these parts. When you fear or deny a part of yourselves, believing it undesirable, it often surfaces in your relationships.

When you least expect it the dark regions that we block out of our conscious awareness erupt with feelings of guilt, anger, and shame. These blockages are formed by the defense mechanisms we build up in childhood. As hard as you try you can't eliminate these toxic attitudes and behavior entirely. None of us is perfect.

Carl Jung talks at length on the subject of the dark side of the ego, called the shadow. He says the shadow is a moral problem that challenges the whole ego-personality, for no one can be conscious of the shadow or integrate it into the personality without considerable moral effort. You must accept the dark parts of yourself as present and real. When stirred the shadow produces an emotional response with a decidedly obsessive or possessive quality.

A great astrologer, Liz Green, in a book called *Relating,* said that what you find, when you look into how relationships work, is that most of what goes on in a relationship is unconscious, because most of what we are remains unconscious. The mystery of why you are attracted to a certain type of person, why you begin a relationship in a particular way, why it takes the course it does, and why you encounter the particular problems you must cope with is less a mystery when you realize that much of what you call attraction and repulsion is really based on unconscious qualities within yourself.

Remember, emotion is something that happens to you. When it erupts from the shadow part of the personality where it was hiding all the time, the reaction that is created the most is a need for control. This is when the challenge of your sign takes over and your ethical judgment is weak. By being aware of these patterns and developing a willingness to search for new approaches, you learn how to minimize the toxic experiences you inflict on yourself and others, as well as those that you allow others to inflict on you.

Remember that your partner reflects you and your inner nature. Many times a darker version of yourself, the shadow part of your personality, will come in to court you. Remember the old folk song: "The frog went a-courting and he did ride / With a knife and a pistol by his side / he asked Miss Mousy to be his bride." Poor Miss Mousy thought she was going out on a nice date. Watch out! The feeling of familiarity and exhilaration that you feel when you enter a new relationship could lead to your worst nightmare.

Defining Your Emotions

The voice of your emotions reflects your intent.

If you look deeply at your hurts and disappointments you can see where your intentions have been thwarted. When you realize that emotions are currents of feelings that come through you, that they aren't who you are, you can detach enough to calmly sort out what needs to be done to return to a positive life path. Accepting yourself as an emotional being helps you accept your partner's emotions as well and gives you patience when his response isn't what you pictured.

These definitions can be used by any Sun sign. Each sign may act out a different reaction but the feelings come from the same base.

Your emotions have important information that can tell you where your fears lie. If you pay attention to what you are feeling you can trace your emotional turmoil back to the beginning when you first felt that way and see which intention was thwarted. In all my years of astrology counseling I have found that we all have the same hurts and disappointments and our biggest fear is that we won't be loved.

Your emotions that can be a tool for self-knowledge and healing if you understand what the true feeling is behind them.

- Anger: Unexpressed hurt. Loss of control over others and an attempt to regain it.

- Confusion: The laziness of mind that precedes a decision. An uncomfortable stage before making up your mind.

- Fear: An imaginary experience of injury and loss that has not yet occurred.

- Fantasy: An escape technique. Going into your imagination to hide from reality.

- Guilt: Indulging in feelings over a past situation in order to avoid taking action now.

- Hurt: To have a deep wound, place blame, and deny the responsibility for your own expectations.

- Loneliness: Placing responsibility for your happiness on someone else.

- Rationalizing: A technique to escape emotion.

- Rejection: An unsuccessful attempt to gain approval.

- Resentment: Anger and hurt.

- Self-pity: Indulging in helplessness as a luxury.

- Depression: Unexpressed negative emotions, such as guilt, anger, or hurt.

- Shame: Debilitating belief with no hope of redemption.

- Shyness: Waiting for someone else to tell you you're okay.

- Worry: Trying to control the future. Suppressing yourself to keep from preparing for a situation.

Every honest relationship is an active process. First there must be a commitment based on a mutual desire for a relationship in which the lives of both partners are significantly intertwined. Secondly there must be mutual trust or you are just wasting your time.

When you find yourself confused and upset by your own actions or those of your partner, this is a simple process for getting in touch with your emotions. This may be done alone or with your partner. By being able to talk freely with each other your intimacy bond grows and you open a new level of love and trust.

1. Recognize that you are emotional.

2. Use the previous list to pinpoint and define your emotion.

3. Accept responsibility for that emotion. When did you feel this way the last time? Before that?

4. What triggered this feeling? Describe the situation physically to your partner. What did you see? What did you hear? What do you think? How do you feel?

5. Behind every emotion there is a belief. What is it?

6. What are you getting from your emotion? What feels bad and what feels good about it?

7. How can you change your belief? Contemplate, then write an affirmation that creates a new response.

8. What are you willing to do to change this situation? What are you willing to give up? What do you want to hold on to?

If you are sharing this information with your partner it's important for you to follow through the script without inter-ruption. Then it's your partner's turn. After both of you have shared your thoughts and feelings, give each other the chance to say what you're willing to do to solve this situation. If there is no immediate resolution, give it a little time. If your partner isn't ready to, then do this exercise by yourself. The point is *not* to be right but to share and learn from your emo-tional experience.

March 21–April 20

Aries in Love

ELEMENT:	Fire
QUALITY:	Cardinal
PLANET:	Mars
STONE:	Diamond
COLOR:	Red
ANIMAL:	Ram
FLOWER:	Poppy
LOVE WORDS:	Fly me to the moon

Gift — Vibrancy and Allure
Challenge — Self-Absorption

When an Aries Falls in Love

Aries is a cardinal sign in the fire element; it is the self-starter of the zodiac.

You are born seeking out stimulating situations and know intrinsically that in these peak experiences your heart opens with excitement and your soul weaves its divinity into your life.

Your romance will be a very thrilling experience or you're out of there as quickly as possible. On the other hand, when you enter into someone's life, it's quite an event for them. You generate sparks and a lot of action. How can anyone resist your enthusiasm, your beautiful hawklike eyes, and your exercise-honed body? Your self-confidence and natural joie de vivre encourage action and push anything that's unimportant to the wayside.

Mars, Aries's ruling planet, consists of a circle, a symbol for love and completeness, with an arrow attached on the side. The arrow is pointing up, slightly to the right, directing the circle toward the right or the conscious side. Mars is the symbol of directing love (the circle) into conscious action (arrow). When Arians want something they take action. Remember the arrow that is pointing up also indicates looking toward heaven or God's will.

Classically Mars rules the masculine—desire in motion. In medical books, the symbol for Mars is also the symbol for the male sex organ. By having such a dynamic ruler Arians are endowed with competitive and leadership talents.

Aries is the first sign in the zodiac, the sign of spring and new growth. In a personal way it represents the birth of conscious awareness. It rules the head, which houses the brain. Aries people are very smart and often they don't like to get a classical education. They like to develop their own ideas. With their strong will and razor-sharp concentration they can make it to the top without a college degree. If their individual chart suggests it, however, they can excel in school, easily going to the head of the class. Many Arians are intellectuals yet they are spurred on by their desire to learn something new and rarely get verbose. An Aries in any position is extremely motivated to win and they will pioneer any subject in which they're interested.

Aries was the only child of Jupiter and Hera, his wife, although Jupiter fathered perhaps five hundred children. Aries never married; he preferred to show his bravery in battle. He had a famous liaison with Venus, the goddess of love. The planets Mars and Venus in the zodiac are the rulers of opposite signs, Aries and Libra. Aries is in a balancing act with Libra. This opposing viewpoint is a constant challenge. There is always a peaceful Libra just under cover in your nature. Sooner or later you have to accept the blessings of your opposite sign, and when you do your fiery nature settles down and your life is better.

Aries, whose father was Jupiter, and Venus, whose father was Uranus, parented Eros and the desire for erotic love was born on earth. Aries people have a difficult time distinguishing between love and passion. When you are united with someone on earth by true devotion, then this love is a seed. As it grows you experience the fruit of this affection in the future. The key word here is *unite*. If winning is your motivation and all you want to do is pursue erotic love, there is no fruit to experience.

It's the promise and possibility of love that's important to an Aries. When someone comes into your life, no matter what the circumstances, even if you've known the person for years, it is a moment full of potential and passion. I've come to believe that relationships are fated. You can't force Eros to appear. When the lightning bolt of attraction appears, it is one of the most exhilarating experiences of a lifetime. An Aries loves this part of a relationship and tries to keep it going for a long as possible. There is a lot of vulnerability in that moment, which adds fuel to the fire. The race is on.

Your Nature Is Fiery and Aggressive

One of the biggest gifts we have in life is to madly crave something or someone, to set our sights on something that delights and intrigues us.

Warren Beatty, the actor and an Aries, when asked what he wanted most in life, said, "To be interested." Without desire and longing we would all be emotionally dry and listless. As a fire sign, which rules the feeling function, you like to encompass the greatest possibilities; an almost consuming interest has to be there. It is important for you as an Aries feeler to experience life dramatically. You want to approach the essence of a situation and plunge. It doesn't matter to you if its a positive or negative situation as long as you are impacted by it and experience excitement.

Other people observe your reactive ways and wonder why you get so excited and carried away by such simple things. You go on impulses—then you can't put into words how you've come to your conclusions. This happens because Aries is a masculine sign that is ruled by the left brain or linear process. When you are activated by your heart's desire, you jump over into right-brain activity of nonlinear processing, which produces the reaction but not the words. There are always two sides to existence, the side you see and the side you don't see. The first side is obvious information—it's a quick read; the second is beyond structures of time, space, and the mind. This is where magic and miracles reside. You instinctively reach out for this experience, even if you don't fully grasp what you are doing. You are capable of understanding things that are not obvious to others.

Many Aries are mystics. The most famous Arian type of all was Moses, the great avatar of the Aries age, who saw the burning bush. He also talked to God (*definitely* a right-brained process) and received the Ten Commandments.

You love to be surprised and you like to be intrigued. Your love life is a guessing game. You go after the hard to get and take on tremendous challenges.

When a quickening of interest enters your life you come alive with joy and satisfaction—you experience the creative part of the human condition and the most satisfying. As a feeler the beginning will always be the most important part and the more dramatic the better. Until the spark ignites, there is no love story. I sometimes think that people don't appreciate the power of that instant of realization. It is a miracle, a blessing from the universe. This spark is everything to you Arians.

Aries likes to be in constant motion. Rarely do you sit around and wait for love to walk in the door. When someone matches the picture of who you want, you spontaneously give chase. It is your nature to pursue. It is so thrilling to you, the outcome is insignificant. All this action without mental processing keeps you energized and thrilling. You like the act of pursuit to the point of totally ignoring the outcome of this act. What matters most to you is to act again and again. It's risk and fun not to know the outcome. A compelling need for self-gratification also colors all of your decisions and is obviously detrimental to how your partner feels. As a result Aries have a reputation of being selfish when it may not be the case at all. The question is, what are you going to do when you get there and they say yes? What are you going to do when you get what you want is the big question. What do you have planned for phase two? It may be that in some deep-seated way you want to lose; then you're free to start again. Think about it.

Relating on a Soul Level

Aries's gift is vibrancy and allure.

When an Aries comes into the room all eyes turn. Your vital good looks attract attention wherever you are and your alluring aura enchants the opposite sex. Your opposite sign Libra influences you greatly. Aries rules the interest and the beginning of a relationship whereas Libra rules commitment. Underneath your aggressive and independent personality, you are a romantic.

As an Aries your life is lived in pursuit of love, and therein lies the problem. For an Aries the act of love is paramount but committing is not so easy. Try to determine the possible success of your relationship. Don't get so involved in what you want to see when you know in your heart of hearts no reality is there. Take your time and think it through; request feedback, allow for due process. Your thoughts must complement your actions. Try to distinguish between what you want and what you really need. The ability to compromise the two is a sign of maturity. True courage has patience. To reach your goal of love you have to risk, yes, but not in a left-brained masculine way. Love is a whole-brained operation.

Open your heart to both your intuitive and rational selves to develop self-control, compromise, and moderation. When you are in touch with your soul power, your heart is open. To maintain this state of consciousness, there is a need to slow down and be thoughtful.

These four tips might help you achieve the love you want.

1. Change your perspective on how to get your needs met.

2. You can have what you want but you need to have a more mature attitude about what you need and want.

3. Meet your partner creatively, allow your soul to respond vitally and fully.

4. Practice cooperation, meeting your partner in the real terms of their individual needs.

By changing your perspective and with a lot of self-control you can be thrilled with what you see, and decide to stay.

A great twentieth-century astrologer, Dane Rudhyar, talks about the difficult task of discrimination for an Aries. He says that you must be adaptable, yet retain the purity and total integrity of your vision and ideals. You must accept detours, yet not lose the direction of the goal. You must be understandable and acceptable to those who need spiritual arousal, yet not distort or lower the message. By lifting up your own consciousness you can operate in the past, present, and future. You must learn to be considerate and kind to everyone, yet uncompromisingly true to your own spirit—such are the problems that the creative Aries person will constantly meet in one form or the other.

Rudhyer later goes on to say that ultimately it's you, Aries, who must come to realize that your activity, if it is to be true to the law of the spirit, must be conditioned by compassion rather than the sheer joy of creative release. Also the independent spirit means nothing if it is not joined with consideration of others.

Antoine de Saint-Exupéry, in his beautiful book *The Little Prince,* said, "Love does not consist of gazing at each other, but in looking outward in the same direction." This is a perfect blueprint of an Arian in an Aquarian age relationship.

Blocking Yourself from Love

Arians are a restless bunch of rams. You often see what you want to see, and more times than not your eyes focus on what is coming over the horizon.

Once ignited an unevolved Aries sets out to conquer all. There is a tendency to live in the future with hopes and dreams full of fantasy. With so much expectancy the object of your affection may not look so good closer up. You need to slow down a little and learn to be more discerning about your requirements. Aries see love as a conquest and when the unsuspecting object succumbs, interest fades. Why? With your challenge of self-absorption, it's the quest that's exciting and when your love is returned, interest dwindles and the conquest is over. Whetting your appetite makes you feel more alive to seek the unusual and hard to get. In your quest for the new, the different, and the exciting you are constantly scanning the horizon looking for new fuel, even though you may have attracted someone wonderful—just not someone who meets your predetermined criteria.

Excitement junkies need extreme stimulation to motivate their crusade—that is, until they find that good communication and patience can be equally challenging. There are people out there who are vital and enthusiastic about life and make rewarding partners.

Relationships are a tremendous challenge for everyone, but for you they are a major issue. With vibrancy and allure as your soul gifts, you have the ability to attract relationships like moths to a flame. Many a heart has been broken as you walk on by and ignore the very fire that you've ignited. You are held accountable for your behavior karmically and sooner or later, as the old saying goes, "What goes around comes around." You must take responsibility for what you say and do. Relationships are more than entertainment.

When you start a path of intimacy with another person it is exciting, a process of discovery and a way to become more conscious. You have the ability to make your partner feel incredibly special. You need someone who has a strong sense of self, who radiates a strong passionate nature, and who has a sense of purpose in life. The person must have a sense of adventure and a desire to move forward in life. In other words, you attract yourself. Your partner may also feel he will lose himself in a relationship and withdraw. What a blow to your ego; he may even beat you to withdrawal. A certain amount of maturity must be attained before you can attract and maintain a positive relationship. You must look at the paradox of your urgent need for a relationship and your need for absolute freedom. By learning your opposite sign Libra's gift of cooperation you end up giving a relationship more time to develop. In learning to give sans self-serving motives, you will attract someone who gives to you.

1. You must slow down and look at what this relationship brings into your life. Be realistic. Is it good for you or not?

2. Always wanting to win love shows that your self-esteem is based on what others think.

3. Remember that love is not a target. When you have a loving heart you attract what is best for

you and your love life isn't such a challenge to
you.

4. It is wise to know that the most important relationship you ever have is with yourself. Work
   at knowing yourself and what you truly need
   and want in a relationship.

You like to win. This ambitious attitude often puts you in
the contrary position of always wanting to be right. The
irony is that because of your intuitive nature you are right a
lot. The risk of going beyond that place of safety where you
are totally in control, to opening to someone else's opinions
definitely isn't comfortable. Intimacy forces us to take off our
masks. You like being the instigator; you have the courage to
give up your warrior ways and lay down the sword. The path
of love is a solace if you listen to your heart.

Constantly in motion, with all your strength and enthusiasm, you can wear yourself down. Mars rules the adrenal
glands and with continual stress you become depleted. The
constant pressure of pursuit isn't necessarily romantic even
though it may make you feel relevant. You will still be just as
vital if you are relaxed. Achieving and acquiring are exagger-
ated traits of the world we live in now and it's easy for you to
get caught up in them.

To be soul-conscious you must become more aware of the
subtleties. By adapting to the truth of the moment you can
seek out what's best for all concerned. This takes considerable patience. In other words, get over your desire for instant
gratification and see the bigger picture. You don't have to lose
your own vision or your motivation but you mustn't waste so
much in action and lose your energy on inconsequential
schemes. It takes great courage (heart) to be present in the
moment and process your thoughts and feelings.

Another reason Aries go in and out of relationships so
quickly is the tendency to leave when the going gets difficult.
You may be afraid that in loving someone you will have to

give up your identity. Or because your desire is so intense, you want to maintain the feeling that you can't live without the other person; you're really addicted to your own melodrama. Remember the circle of love is the basis for the action in the symbol for Mars. The circle denotes an unending cycle, a marriage of heaven and earth. A commitment can be as rewarding as the first glow of passion, if you change your gears.

Aries prefer the fast track in love and career; it's hard for you to stay put in normal situations. One wonders if your enthusiasm is based on nonreality. Your arrogance can drag you down when things aren't as great as you thought they were. There are checkpoints in courtship when you have to face what's really there. It may not be like you pictured it.

When things slow down with life's gravity (it does happen eventually) you lose interest. You like to be on the cutting edge—creating new goals, conquering new territory. This burning intensity makes you feel so alive. You can keep up this fervor only so long. Your partner is an ordinary person with normal problems, just like yourself. With an Aries when the illusion is over, the soaring feeling drops to zero. It's been said many times that familiarity breeds contempt, and if the love isn't appreciated, the end is close in sight. True love is a precious gift and must be honored.

An Aries Love Story

If You've Got It, You Don't Want It!

Many Aries men and women come into my office in emotional frustration about their love lives. Either they love someone who doesn't return their affection or they have succeeded in winning someone's heart and they feel trapped. A beautiful Aries client came to me for years. She met a wonderful man (whose appearance I had predicted) and very excitedly came to me to see if their charts were compatible. There are certain aspects in a natal chart that show what is compatible and what could be problematic in a relationship. In this case their charts were very compatible, the hard aspects looked like they could be worked out, so I helped her with a wedding date even though I thought they shouldn't hurry. It's a good rule of thumb to know each other for at least eighteen months to two years, a complete Mars cycle. She had only known him for five months but wanted to marry quickly. This approach to romance is very common with the feeling type.

I have learned that if a situation is karmic, there is no way to learn but through the experience itself. Years later people call me and say they are just now able to really hear what I told them years before. Astrology therapy is an evolving process.

A year later she came back for me to look at their charts. She wanted a divorce. It wasn't that she didn't love this man, she just felt that she was missing out on life. Her company had offered her a chance to move to Europe and she was going to take it. Her poor husband was in shock. He was confused and bewildered, trying to figure out what had gone wrong. The truth is he wasn't at fault. The snag in their relationship was that she was in love with adventure and couldn't settle for an everyday lifestyle. She had immaturely assumed that marriage was the end all for her and had found out she was wrong.

Unfortunately when an Aries relationship hits a snag it's a quick good-bye. Remember, every problem has a solution. Even if the solution is an ending of the relationship you must take time for closure. A change of attitude with a willingness to communicate sometimes even heals the rift. By releasing your compelling intensity and your narrow-minded passion for independence, your perspective is broadened and you become more tolerant. What is being surrendered is not the self or the soul, which is your true nature, but the desire of the Aries ego to remain separate and in control. This fear of loss of autonomy is the basis for your challenge of self-absorption.

When the beautiful young Aries began to mature she looked back on her earlier behavior with regret. After some very difficult years she could see that her problem was patience, trust, and intimacy. She was afraid of being controlled by love and had given up a very special person with her compulsive behavior.

Your Most Authentic Self

It takes real courage to make a total commitment.

When you recognize that you can't control passion, that ardor comes from your very soul and it can't be entirely satisfied by anyone or anything, you are free of love addiction. Passion and surrender are equal parts of a relationship. It's also important to remember that the most important relationship you have is with yourself. That relationship comes first and must be in good order for a courtship to work out.

The young woman in our story was restless. Love is very special. It's important to give it a chance. An Aries always needs to take time to consider the facts of the situation from an objective viewpoint.

Katharine Hepburn, a Taurian in love with an Arian—Spencer Tracy—once said in an interview, "Love means total interest. If things get rough you shift your position to make it work." And she should know. It took a lot of excitement, change, and diversity to keep these two signs together, and they were for twenty-seven years.

But how do you stay interested enough to do this? That's an Arian dilemma. How do you lose your insularity and blend with others? The answer is to look again. When you reassess the situation, what you want may be what you have already.

Our Aries good-bye girl acknowledged her patterns of fear and denial, which had made it impossible for her to have a satisfying relationship, and after a lot of pain and real suffering she was ready to be transformed. She realized that she didn't have to chase after everything that stirred her feelings. Love doesn't have to be a peak experience every day. Your true interest opens many doors of exploration. If you let your passion move freely, you will keep finding new forms of expression with your partner. Working on a relationship is an exciting possibility.

Patience means that you take time for your relationship to mature. As your life together unfolds you can find harmony between your feelings and your partner's. Don't project your feelings on others. When you are too intent on getting your own romantic needs met, you rush forward without the consent of your partner. Life always puts you in situations where you are forced to learn how to consider others. Count on it.

I have found that you really can't separate the opposite signs. There is an open door between them. The attributes you need to come into balance are the gifts of Libra. Opposite signs are attracted to each other; it's a comfortable feeling to meet your other half. Inside every Aries is a gracious Libra, just waiting with the patience necessary to slow you down. In love matters the polarity of Aries and Libra brings balance. Opposite the war god Aries is the beautiful and mentally adept goddess Athena, who sprang fully formed from the head of Jupiter. She has the wisdom of the gods. The full process of balancing Aries and Libra within yourself involves seeking love, finding it, thinking it through, and making a commitment. When the balancing is complete your love life improves a thousandfold. Just because Aries is on the instigating side of the matter doesn't take away from the romance.

To be authentically Arian means to be fearless. You have

to take that aggressive energy, temper it, and apply it to projects that are far ranging yet help others as well as yourself. To be truly happy in a relationship you need to have a good relationship with yourself. As long as you are trying to fulfill yourself with others—the chase is on. You start at ground zero, of just being interested—again and again and again.

Taurus in Love

ELEMENT:	Earth
QUALITY:	Fixed
PLANET:	Venus
STONE:	Emerald
COLOR:	Green
ANIMAL:	Cow
FLOWER:	Rose
LOVE WORDS:	Hug me, kiss me, squeeze me

Gift — Magnetism
Challenge — Self-Doubt

When a Taurus Falls in Love

Love is paramount in a Taurian's life and rightly so, with Venus, the planet of love and beauty, as your ruler.

The planet Venus derived her name from the most ancient goddess on earth. She has been given many names in ancient times—Ishtar, Inana, Isis, Hathor, and Ceres. It was in Roman times that she was named Venus, as we know her today. As the goddess of love and pleasure, relationships, harmony, music, and the arts—everything that is beautiful inside and out—is under her tutelage. Beauty is very close to spirit. The great romantic poet John Keats said, "Beauty is truth and truth beauty, that is all ye know on earth and all ye need to know."

Haven't you noticed how very spiritual people have a radiance that makes them beautiful no matter what their age or circumstances. They have found that beauty is not a need, it is an ecstasy. It is available at all times, a soul-enchanted state of joy to those who wish to receive it.

Venus also rules anything that pertains to good taste—food, fragrance, texture, anything that is discerned by the five senses. All of our creative expressions, our sexuality, our passion, our social interactions, our feelings for our loved ones, are Venus ruled and consequently important to Taurus. Venusians are kind, courteous, and refined. As we all have Venus in our natal chart, her placement tells about our ability to love ourselves as well as others. But she is your ruler and nurtures your life with an inordinate ability to attract her grace, love, and beauty in every form. Lucky you; it's your birthright. Enjoy it.

As a Taurian you are capable of great affection and your faithfulness to your loved ones brings enduring relationships. Although you like romance, you want it to be real. Your sign is an earth sign, consequently you are practical and don't go in for idealistic or abstract situations. The love you offer is down to earth with intense feeling. When you fall in love you want your loved one with you, and to love you back with complete passion.

By being so sensual and enticing you naturally draw others to you. You don't have to be alone and if you are, it's your choice. If you find yourself in isolation for too long a time, an emotional clearing of some kind is needed for you to get back into the flow of your truly magnetic gift. It is your nature to build a comfortable space that's safe and secure, and once in a relationship it's your desire to be sentimentally close and physically intimate. Taurus is a sign that is soulful, yet wants to express itself physically. It is through such intimacy that the soul is nourished.

We are told by physicists that it is the mind that constructs reality. Our minds interpret frequencies that are projections from another dimension—a deeper order of existence than we live in, one that is beyond our earthly time and space. There is no lack in this universe. An infinite ocean of possibilities is always there, waiting to be manifested. You are a part of that great hologram, which is as vast as the universe itself. The Hindus refer to this as *akasa,* the one pervading substance that is felt by and unites everyone in the universe. There is no division between your consciousness and this unmanifest matter. The illusion of separation is the result of earthbound thinking. If Icarus in search of God flew too close to the sun, you earthbound Taurians in your search dig too deep in the earth.

In his book *The Teachings of Don Juan,* Carlos Castaneda tells of a task given as part of his initiation. After being told to search a porch for the good and the bad spots, he spends the whole night scooting around on the floor until he feels them out. This story has always reminded me of the advanced sensory perception ruled by Taurus—how Taurians naturally find what is good, soothing, and nurturing to them and know instantly what is not.

Your body is in sync with the very throb of nature and from this grounded position your heart tunes to universal symmetry. Taurus rules the drums that native peoples from all over the world use to empower their rituals and celebrations. Every symphony orchestra uses drums and other percussion instruments to ground the other instruments. Music frees the soul and within the very beingness of every Taurus— the beat goes on. You are the musicologist of the zodiac, many of you have beautiful voices, and rhythm is your joy. Go to a Taurian's house and you'll always find music, whether it's on a tape or from a musical instrument.

Your Nature Is Earthy and Practical

The earth is one of the rulers of Taurus and greatly affects a Taurian's disposition.

The earth's chief characteristic is magnetism. There is an electrical pull on our bodies that forces us to feel our bodies. Your body reacts greatly to this constant pull and it can bring you down emotionally and make you feel tired. This is why Taurus is so slow and looks for comfort more than other signs. Comfortable settling into your own territory, you know you can draw on what you need. You like to create a space and hold on to it; change is hard on you.

You want to return to the original Garden of Eden where there was no shame. Taurus is an earth sign that rules the function of sensing. You desire the purity and innocence of a primal past—the exaltation of the senses and emotions over reason and intellect. But above all else Taurians yearn for unity and wholeness. In your gift of magnetism you want to pull the fragments together, heal the wounds of separation from the divine, and become at one with the universe. Taurians naturally understand that communion with nature is necessary to survival. You know that although love is a feeling it is also the noblest form of knowing. You are a primal being, a basic self personality, and want to be immersed into the sensuality of life.

When you fall in love, you become romance personified and feel an urgent need to merge. Being in a relationship is paramount to your sense of well-being, right alongside your desire to have physical safety and financial abundance. The desire to unite, to absorb another person into your own essence, is constantly on your mind. You don't like to be alone.

The planet Venus rules Libra as well as Taurus but the Taurian Venus is much more voluptuous. There is a decidedly earthy quality to your idea of love. In mythology Venus's birth was a dramatic occasion. She was born motherless from the genitals of Uranus. Remember Venus rose from the sea in a froth of sea foam—part air and water. In astrology the air signs rule the thinking function and the water signs rule the emotions. Venus is not all emotion. Her father was from the sky, which is air. Uranus had married the earth goddess, Gaia. It is the same story told by North American Indians of the marriage of sky father and earth mother. Gaia became angry because Uranus, thinking his children were deformed on earth, was destroying them. Their youngest son, Saturn, the god of time, desiring to please his mother, castrated Uranus and dropped his genitals into the ocean.

Venus seems to be the consolation prize of a battle between the earth, the sky, and time. It could be that her dysfunctional beginnings are what contributes to the lessons in love so prevalent on earth. Since Uranus was timeless and Saturn rules time on earth, after the birth of Venus, the earth became a good home for Venusian qualities. Out of chaos and crisis came the birth of beauty and abundance.

How You Relate on a Soul Level

As the second sign in the zodiac, following Aries' dramatic entrance, it is Taurus that molds action into meaning.

You instinctively know how to get your creature comforts met. Taurians always seem to be able to materialize a cup of tea and a muffin, no matter what the circumstances.

Magnetism is a priceless gift. A Taurus is always able to attract a partner. With your powerful will and the natural instinct to make safe boundaries, you (magically, it seems) form, develop, and advance whatever you need and want in the physical world. But if you have self-doubts about your worthiness or you are in a situation that frightens you, your diseased ego drags you down into a deep sense of helplessness. You create a private hell where no one and nothing can please you or divert you until you become emotionally spent and physically drained. It is then and only then that you grudgingly change your perspective.

You have a deep-seated emotional need to control your environment and hold on for dear life to what seems safe at the time; you can trap yourself in a world so narrow that your creative energy is limited. When you've made a romantic choice it's difficult to leave even if the relationship is intolerable.

When your imagination is active, it is not a purely mental process, for you are inseparable from your biological processes. Your emotions and feeling are there to guide you. Your Taurian sensitivity gives you the ability to sense the subtleties that connect the mind and body. There is a resonance between the two, but when you are afraid of losing your physical comfort, in emotional turmoil, you grab hold of the status quo. The old saying "The streets of hell are familiar" describes your compulsive search for security at any cost.

Taurus is a sign of survival. You have the power to sustain the worst blows, and you're never down very long. With your gift of manifestation you can always magnetize a new relationship or job or friend, or anything else for that matter. But when it's time to let go of something or someone you can go into a downward spiral of compulsive reaction that keeps you holding on till hell freezes over.

It is Taurus that rules the function of unfolding these waves of energy into the world of objects and sequential time. You are gifted with an inherent potential for abundance. If you focus on insufficiency and inadequacy, you shut the door to this great source that reaches past the limited mind into fulfilling your every need. You must understand that at a deep level you are inseparable from the flow of nature and there is no division between the mental and physical worlds. You attract what you think. Thoughts create matter and form follows function. What you are imaging will soon be reality.

Heaven always hears you so be careful of what you ask for. What you desire, even if it's stuffed way down in the subconscious, is slowly being formed into the material.

The certainty that we own a little piece of the universe was driven home to me when I read the following quote from the Course in Miracles: "God of himself, would be incomplete without me." Contemplating the words, boundaries faded and I was overwhelmed at the capacity for freedom that we all have. Then my first sense of tremendous power was quickly followed by a sense of humbleness to the responsibility we all have to each other. Quantum physics says the very same thing: if one particle of the universe was removed, the universe would collapse. Nothing can be taken away—but it can be transformed. You are an important and vital part of the universe. How do you want to use this incredible energy?

Blocking Yourself from Love

When love goes wrong, a mood settles over you like a fog.

You imagine that you are totally abandoned and the universe has singled you out to be alone. I always suggest to you Taurians that when you are emotionally despondent you need to take a reality check. Have a good cry, sleep on it, and tend to it tomorrow. This saves a lot of relationships from going up in flames in a Taurian drama. Taurus is the sign that rules theater and music. If you want passion and drama in your life go to Broadway or the opera. Let Betty Buckley and Pavarotti make it worth your while. Beautiful music soothes your very soul.

Woe be it to anyone who tries to move you, change you, or take anything from you, particularly when you're not in a good position to control the outcome. The old chestnut, "A bird in the hand is worth two in the bush," is your motto. To a Taurus, the existing arrangement seems to have more value and to be much safer than any future position.

Taurus is a sign that rules the animal instinct. The unknown is frightening to your aboriginal instincts of survival. There is a tendency to always be in dread of attack from the outside. When shifts inevitably come, unless you have developed a sense of safety within yourself, you become alarmed; then very quickly, the sense of well-being that makes you so charming disappears.

It is your gift to attract love as well as anything else that you need. You have a very sexual nature. A Taurus desires strong, intense, as well as long-term and sustaining sexual expression.

With your magnetic and sexual nature there is a strong desire to nest and have a family. If this isn't the case, you are still nursing hurt and anger from past experiences. Letting go of the past is tied into your challenge of self-doubt. By setting up situations where you are constantly in control, a lot of energy is wasted and pretty soon you're alone again. By being overly cautious and exasperatingly deliberate you fend off the love and support you so desperately need. By learning how to listen to others objectively, to hear their needs and support their development, you will attract someone who does this for you and who does not want to control or limit you. In the world today, when changes are coming so fast, you are forced to find a broader base of comfort and safety.

Ending a romance can send you spinning into a feeling of rejection when that couldn't be further from the truth. Instead of realizing the relationship has real flaws and moving on to new and more beneficial situations, you doggedly want to hold on. When the relationship ends, it is very difficult for you. You don't like to give up anything that has held meaning and value in your life, even if you only project meaning and value onto it. To hold on to the envisioned stability at any cost causes great resentment and anger, which eventually becomes very explosive and damaging to both you and your partner.

The fight or flight syndrome of your instinctive nature takes you on a merry ride. Your reactive behavior stirs up useless forms of control such as ranting, raging, or just running off and hiding, then your energy is diminished and a sense of helplessness colors your decisions. Yet when you are comfortable and feel safe with someone you are sweetness and light itself. You are "the little girl with the curl" in the old nursery rhyme: when you are good you are very, very good, but when you are bad you are horrid.

To create the empty vessel that magnetizes the future, you must take the time to process the past and allow a healing to take place. And by bringing the wisdom from past experiences into your next relationship there is hope of creating something wiser and more lasting. When you can take responsibility for your part of the dysfunction and become "the sadder but wiser guy" there is hope for the future. But heal you will, when you let go of the past.

Your goal is to make life rich and fulfilling, and you treasure what you have. Yet the responsibility of possessions weighs heavily on your heart, until you realize that you are great not because of what you own but because of how you use what you have. Being so earthbound with all the chaos that prevails in that dimension, there is a deep inner fear of loss. Love being taken from you is a recurring fear you have to deal with. Also behind this urgent need to hold on to what you perceive as yours is the fact that you like to be the sole proprietor of your space. You're the bull and you want control of the pasture. You must come to terms with the fact that there is a lot of responsibility attached to ownership.

Assets must be used with the highest integrity. Total identification with what you possess limits your freedom. Yes, you must value what you have, take care of it, and use it properly, or the way of nature takes over and it disintegrates. If you want to go to the deepest level of this dilemma you have to finally realize that we truly don't ever own anything, but things can own us if we are not watchful. There is a universal law that says, "When you let go of something that truly has meaning and value, something much better comes in its place."

Love's Sweet Song

I have a Taurus client who came in for an appointment and the first thing out of her mouth was, "My relationships never work out." And it was true.

In courtship she could never get past the early dating stages. She had never really been in love. She was isolated in a frozen emotional position, a prison of her own fear of rejection. She never let down her defenses. As much as she wanted to go through all the phases of courtship and commitment with a wonderful person, she couldn't see what was obvious to others. She was a difficult person to be with. She gave the impression of wanting to fight, not make love.

My heart went out to her because she has been hurt by this dilemma and hasn't been able to see what she needed to change. As my mother used to say, "Looks weren't her problem." She was exceptionally beautiful. Her unrest made her interesting; when she came into a room, there was a ripple of excitement, but her energy didn't wear well. Frustration kept her on an emotional edge, and she didn't acknowledge what she innately had to offer. She couldn't see herself at all. Her natural gifts of beauty and magnetism were ignored and she chose to think of herself as rejected and alone. Poor Taurus, longing to find peace of mind—it eluded her. Her soul was pained.

There were a lot of opportunities for dates, but guys didn't stay long. The impression she gave to others was that she wanted a challenge. She was daring love. When she was shown love, she doubted it. This created a variety of dramatic responses—from power struggles to browbeating. She felt she had to please her partners or control them. This dilemma confused her and made her angry.

She felt like she couldn't win; she was either a trophy or an opponent. After she had a reading and began to understand her challenge of self-doubt she began to change her perspective. She quit watching herself and became who she really was: a vulnerable and sensitive human being. The defenses came down and her natural gift of magnetism started to work.

Of course this lack of trust wasn't easy to let go of. It took some time. The hurts from her past had to be healed and released. One good thing about a Taurus is that when they get the right idea, the rest follows very quickly. She is still feisty and vibrant, but there is a softer look. She is more patient and she has learned how to be happy with her own company. She is creating a loving space inside and there is no doubt that she will have what she wants. She's let go of the mistrust that magnetized more mistrust.

As her values changed she attracted men with better values. Now her energy is used to accommodate a relationship. The last I heard she was dating one of her old boyfriends. Earlier she had blown him off as a wuss. With her new eyes she could see what she couldn't before. The next time I hear from her, I know she'll be engaged; she's in a nesting pattern in her chart. Life's like that; there is a flow when you quit fighting it.

Your Most Authentic Self

When someone enters your world all of your attention is focused on the new object of your affection.

Your desire is to master love and this takes you into inner conflict. You are in your element in a love affair and the challenges it unfolds create the drama you so love. You desire to merge with love's sacred dimension and at the same time there is a bothersome undercurrent of detachment.

Dating is sort of like scooting around on Carlos Castaneda's floor, trying to find the "good spot." If you have the right attitude you have a better chance of finding what you are looking for. You have the charisma that is needed to find a partner and you have instincts for the truth. Be patient and you will find what you want.

Your life experience is enriched with love's passion, but also with the frustration and pain that often follows the vulnerability of love. This is unsettling to you and keeps you keyed up and tense. To have a good relationship takes time and effort. You have to understand your own inner conflict or you will project it off onto your partner. Then you have the choice of being rageful—or finally getting it, so you can start a new path with a broader base of choices, not so much blame, and a sense of true worthiness that attracts all that is good.

Gemini in Love

ELEMENT:	Air
QUALITY:	Mutable
PLANET:	Mercury
STONE:	Citrine
COLOR:	Yellow
ANIMAL:	Monkey
FLOWER:	Daisy
LOVE WORDS:	Do you love me?
	Do you love me not?

Gift — Delight
CHALLENGE — Diversion

When a Gemini Falls in Love

Gemini rules communication, the most vital part of a relationship, giving you a jump start in attracting a partner.

Forever young with an abundance of energy you are a delight to be around. Your enchanting conversation and imaginative ideas stimulate all who are lucky enough to come into your orbit. What fun! What interesting news! It's entertaining to be around the verve and endless talent you Geminis possess. No wonder you have your choice in partners when you are seeking a relationship.

You are a superb conversationalist and are never, I mean never, at a loss for words. In fact, if you meet someone and

find yourself engaged in a endless conversation there is probably some Gemini in their chart too. Gemini is affectionate
and fond of home and children. Actually your sign rules siblings, aunts, uncles, cousins, and neighbors. A very folksy
sign, a people person, you love having someone to share your
ideas. You choose a mate based essentially on his or her ability to mentally stimulate you. Not to say you're not physical;
just the opposite, you are as physically active as you are mentally fertile. Most Geminis are extremely agile and often excel
in sports, and let's not leave out dancing! In my mind's eye the
symbol I see for Gemini is a group in perfect harmony—like
the Rockettes in Radio City Music Hall—dancing across the
stage in endless multiplicity. Each beautiful, moving together
in unison—dancing up a storm.

Gemini, remember, you are *more than one*, in fact, there
are at least sextuplets (there could be a whole army) inside
your lithe and flexible body. Each one enormously charming
and each one making choices. In a reading I always tell Geminis that it's time for *all of them* to take a majority vote or
their life will be pulled apart. Each facet going off in a different
direction can only bring confusion and there won't be enough
energy left to make decisions. There is such an excitement for
life that you have interest in a large variety of subjects and
take on myriad projects. It's not to say that you don't have
your down time, but it never lasts very long. You can count
on that, yet there's an enigma to your personality. Behind all
that charm and entertaining sense of humor, the question
your partner most often asks is, "Will the *real* you stand up?"
It's hard to get a solid fix on who you are. This isn't like *The
Three Faces of Eve* necessarily, with the good and bad traits,
it's more like a group of totally different personalities, each
talented in a different way, struggling to do their thing.

Gemini's proclivity for constantly searching for variety is
better understood if you know the attributes of the planet
Mercury, your planetary ruler. In ancient Greece he was the
messenger of the gods as well as the ruler of good fortune

when at the crossroads. On the other hand, he was deemed the maker of mischief for those who lack discrimination. There is an element of the Trickster here. In Native American lore the Trickster is an important aspect of their spiritual hierarchy. It relates to the law of chaos in the universe. Without chaos there would be no surprises, no hope of change for humanity. Choosing new directions is your life lesson. Each choice brings a different lesson and opens the door to a different consequence. It is a wise Gemini who remembers the responsibility of her decisions, at every moment.

Geminis talk to everyone, even the people at the next table, the waiters, anyone that walks by. They don't miss a thing. With your personable nature you meet people everywhere, even on your computer. Geminis love the Internet. Many people with Gemini prevalent in their chart race home after work anxious to hear their computers say, "You've got mail." It isn't even uncommon for you to meet the right mate electronically, and the good news is when you finally decide to get together you'll know a lot about each other already. There is a warning here however: remember some people can talk a good game. It's not always important what a person says or writes—it's what that person does that counts. Writing was very popular at the end of the nineteenth century when people lived so far apart written correspondence was necessary. It seems we're back to that even though your pen pal may be just down the street. With so few ways to meet the opposite sex these days the Web has opened up a whole new form of socializing. You fare well in writing notes with your glib way of expressing yourself and you can write about your feelings more easily than you can speak.

Geminis love *love*. You hate to be alone and are always looking for a relationship. There is a deep-seated longing to be with someone that keeps you looking for a partner. Perhaps it's the need to find your lost twin. You are like the proverbial bicycle built for two. You take relationships seriously and give them more time and thought than any other area of your life. Often you have two or more best friends, and a significant other is always on your mind. When you meet someone you like there is an instant reaction and you like to have an immediate response from the person. Gemini falls in love very quickly but needs to realize the difference between love and like. No one falls in love on the first date, even if they think so. They're just lucky *like* turns into *love*. My advice is always to slow down and let time work on the relationship. No one is so intuitive that they know everything about someone in one night. *Slow down,* however, isn't in your vocabulary. You must learn patience. Still it takes someone very interesting with lots of energy to keep up with you. You lose interest very quickly and when you do you're out of there. No dillydallying with the twins.

Your Nature Is Intelligent and Thoughtful

Gemini is an air sign and rules the thinking process.

As a thinker, you take all the life experiences that come to you and try to uncover an underlying pattern of logic. You have a pressing need to relate to a preconceived framework of ideas. By collecting information logically, weighing one thing against another, you form a philosophy of your own. In his book on psychological types Carl Jung describes the thinker as someone with a highly developed mind, a sense of fairness, and the ability to assess information from an impersonal standpoint.

The thinking function is the most removed from our instinctual nature. We have perhaps overdeveloped this function in the last three hundred years. Now as we move into the Aquarian age ruled by an air sign we have to be careful we don't become so isolated from the our feelings that we lose our way on our evolutionary path of liberation of the soul. At this time in history we've become so overly individualized and self-seeking that we often lose sight of the principles that are a positive part of the thinking function. By being overly competitive we lose our compassion. The only answer is to get in touch with your inner feelings and let your decisions reflect what's best for all—and remember, you're included in that process.

Astrologically, with Gemini as an air sign and Mercury ruling the mind you are a thinker of the highest order. If you ask a Gemini how they feel they'll answer with how they think. You've been called mercurial—there's no one mentally faster or more agile than you Geminis. Your ruler, Mercury, is the fastest-moving planet in our solar system. The only other body out there that goes faster is the Moon, and many of you have personal planets, your Sun, your ascendant, your Moon, in Cancer, which is the sign right after Gemini. Your behavior is responsive to your environment, but remember, when you speed through life it's easy to miss bits of information, maybe something important. That's a Gemini dilemma—how to slow down and see what's really happening, then patiently process the facts. You need to find a point of mental, emotional balance within yourself. As a Gemini, each moment of your life is exceptionally full of potential and it makes a lot of difference who you're with. Your thinking is very influenced by your partner. Gemini wants to please the situation and you feel it's your duty to be the one to make changes. It's easy for you, you're flexible, you have the energy for it, "Why not?" Still, it's not always necessary for you to make a move; sometimes the best decision is to stay put. By being too flexible you can lose the power of the moment, and by vacillating you can cause a great deal of trouble and pain, and that's not funny.

With Mercury being the ruler of good fortune at the crossroads there is a deeper message that needs exploring. In olden days the crossroads were often a very dangerous place—people could make wrong turns or be beset by robbers; there were many possible consequences that couldn't be controlled.

As a master of the crossroads you can always find the right solution to move you forward on your life's path. The symbol of the twins was chosen, I'm sure, to show the balancing of the practical mind with inner feeling. Your ability to slow down, listen to yourself, and make decisions is excellent. It is your karma and your gift.

Gemini rules multiple births. My astrology teacher in Dallas broadened that piece of information for me when he said that Gemini not only ruled the twins but also ruled the concept of *more than one,* the concept of multiplicity. You're not one, you're a crowd. You learn early to separate yourself—one kind of behavior at work, another at home, someone else at a party; you slip in and out of your different personas without much awareness of what you are doing. It can get very confusing for your partner. Maybe the reason you Geminis have so many relationships in one lifetime is to manifest all your other selves.

In a natal chart the signs of the zodiac are distributed around the chart with each sign ruling an area of your life. The area that Gemini rules is where there is the most changeability. If it's on the cusp of the house of career, there will be two or more careers. If it's on the cusp of house of marriage, you may well be married more than once or maybe marry a Gemini. This could be very lucky for you, as two Geminis create an environment that is flexible and interesting, with never a dull moment.

Relating on a Soul Level

Delight is your gift.

The purpose of life is to experience joy and Gemini understands that philosophy. Your basic instinct is to be agreeable and your attitude is basically congenial. Gemini is an air sign with a dynamic and energetic persona. The air signs are thinkers and have a masculine approach to life. You like to take an idea forward and complete it very quickly. Yet because of a tendency to be emotionally fragmented you tend to get overwhelmed. Then all that joy regresses into confusion and your thoughts splinter into a million pieces that helplessly fall on the floor.

As charming and interesting as you are to be with, it's hard to second-guess you. Because of your changeable nature, your love of unprecedented ideas, and your search for diversity, you keep your loved ones guessing. This makes you attractive to the opposite sex; everyone likes to have fun with their partners, and your easygoing personality makes you very pleasant to be with. You are always positive in your thinking and ready to laugh and share your life with someone.

Lucky you with Mercury's blessings, with your youthful approach to life, you are good with people of all ages. You seem to bypass the aging process, stay young-looking, and take on projects at an age that some people might even think is inappropriate. That, of course, is their problem. A Gemini woman wears short skirts and youthful clothes all of her life. A Gemini man often has his tennis racket or golf club in his hand into the golden years, and he can win, too.

You are extremely verbal, language comes naturally to you. Most Geminis start talking very young, then never stop. Each new experience brings on comparison, analysis, and vivid mental images, which further develops your already excellent intellect. As you maneuver through life, your memory is excellent. You make excellent writers. Gemini rules the communications world.

You want to create an eventful and interesting life to delight in. You basically have a positive attitude even when things go wrong. Being very forgiving, you can't stay mad very long. You're the one that says, "Lets not cry over spilled milk." You're ready to move forward without holding a grudge.

Blocking Yourself from Love

If someone asks you how you feel, you are at a loss for words.

Your lesson in life: scattered emotions that come from trying to think your emotions, and your challenge is diversion. There is a tendency to suppress your deeper feelings. You do anything you can to divert the flow back into the positive vein, and yet you have to know that negative thoughts and feeling can't be suppressed or detoured. You like to unemotionally sort them out, categorize them, and move on. But sooner or later your long-suppressed emotions will overflow and make an emotional storm that's worse than it would have been with an earlier recognition. With this tendency to deny unhappy thoughts and feelings there is a buildup of sadness that catches up with you sooner or later. Many Geminis become overly sensitive because of this accumulation of unexpressed emotions.

Without another person around you would be lost. To be really inspired you have to bounce energy off of someone else. Although there is a real tendency here to be like the old song; "If you can't be with the one you love, love the one you're with." As you mature you realize that a new partner every week isn't sustaining to your real nature of wanting to develop a deep and meaningful relationship. The new and different doesn't have to diminish the tried and true; there's room for both experiences. Since Gemini is an air sign, which rules the mind and the thinking function, the core issue at stake here is how you think. Therein lies the sum and substance of your gift of delight and your challenge of diversion. It's your choice of being emotionally scattered and impatient or happy in the present with what is really happening. It takes time to sort out your feelings, but until you do, you jump to mental conclusions and your choices will lack a connection to your deeper needs. This leads you on a merry chase, running away from the pain of confronting your own emotions. Choice is a wonderful thing, but when you're strung out, self-doubt takes over, you become indecisive and can't finish anything.

Your saving grace is the delight you take in life; you love to laugh and have a great sense of humor. Your cheerful attitude takes you far. You're a big tease but never in a mean way.

The little prince in Antoine de Saint-Exupéry's famous little book said, "True love is visible not to the eyes, but to the heart, for the eyes may deceive." Part of your lesson in life is that culturally we are programmed to ignore our emotions. You are taught to achieve, to win, and to hurry up so no one gets ahead of you. What pressure that puts you under. You are the teenager of the zodiac and you don't like to look at the consequences. But your good nature and charming ways can save you just so many times. Perhaps that is why you have had so many jobs, friends, and lovers. This trait of flirting with time, pushing the envelope, is irresistible to you until you wake up to what you're doing. It's sad when friends and relationships of all kinds start to fall away without you knowing why. Yet when you are inspired and trust your feelings, you bring joy and, yes, delight to all around you. When you are scattered and in a hurry you can selfishly, probably unknowingly, take advantage of the ones you love.

In a world that's been programmed for left-brained linear thinking, the right brain, which rules holistic and intuitive knowledge, has been overlooked for thousands of years. You use both sides of the brain equally when it comes to ideas but in the emotional areas of your life you are at a loss. Emotion confuses the issue, holds you back, slows you down. "Why do I feel that way?" is not a question you want to ask. You like the future, not the past. So you try to skirt your feelings and emotions when you can. This delay or denial creates right and left brain separation. The left brain takes over, leading you into a fragmented and isolated lifestyle. You've heard the phrase "alone in a crowd"—it isn't your goal but it can happen.

Intrigue and adventure keep you moving at a fast pace. You neglect your feelings and bypass the valuable information that's stored in your subconscious. Your partner gets upset as you pass by the emotional content of the situation very easily. With such a quick mind and so many interests you can charm anyone you come in contact with but it wears thin after hours of waiting and lame explanations for being late or even totally forgetting your date. Your loved one can grow to resent your scattered ways.

It's easy for you, being in such a hurry and loving every minute of it, to become separated mentally and emotionally. You're not really inconsiderate or insensitive to your partner's needs, but there is always one more call to make or one more place to go before you honor your appointment. "I'll just stop by the drugstore and get a few things," and you show up about twenty minutes late. Again. Since you are the lord of the crossways you have the innate ability to be exactly on time. There is a perfect point at the crossing of any two lines. This power comes when you face your emotional fears of being stopped—or controlled.

A Gemini Love Story

I want you to love me.

Marilyn Monroe was one of the major love goddesses of the twentieth century. Her love life was typical of all Geminis. (Of course we must take into consideration she was emotionally abused in early childhood and many of her choices were colored with a sense of low self-esteem.)

Geminis often present themselves in a way that camouflages the real picture. Looking soft and vulnerable and acting

Gemini in Love | 115

like a dumb blonde sex goddess probably served the times. She certainly had the equipment. Even in this age where skinny models are role models, she still looks good with those few extra pounds. The question is, how did she attract such brilliant, powerful men if she wasn't intelligent herself? I'd say she was a foxy lady and knew how to create herself to achieve her goal, however, her substance abuse to overcome her fears and her lack of self-esteem led her down a path of unhappiness and misery. Geminis don't like boundaries. True to this trait she let no one control her and constantly had people around who served her addictions. What a loss! I wonder if today with so many recovery centers using more advanced techniques if the outcome would have been different.

Finding it hard to make decisions and commitments kept her constantly late, and gossips said that the very punctual Clark Gable had a heart attack and died from the frustration of waiting for her. She promised again and again to show up on time but the desire to speed through life pulled her into a frantic schedule of drugs and alcohol, abusive men, and the ensuing illness such confusion brings. She was a great comedian and left a legacy of great movies that proved a truly beautiful woman can be very funny.

Your Most Authentic Self

Your gift is delight and this joyful resonance is attained when you express some essential part of yourself.

A Gemini always makes time for fun. You never rest on your laurels. No sooner have you accomplished one great feat than you're off planning another. You are a pleasure to spend time with, having the most charming way of presenting yourself and making even the most mundane times stimulating. Your quick mind invigorates and rouses even the most difficult person into making a fresh effort.

You are at your best in an environment that calls for change and variety. You natural desire to happily share with others makes you an excellent companion. When a Gemini has matured out of the tendency to talk incessantly and learns to listen to others, you are able to make wonderful marriages. Your capricious nature settles down and you are more committed than other signs. You always try to make the best of any situation and will go out of your way to make a relationship work.

With so many ideas, so much activity, and so many decisions to make, the most important lesson Gemini deals with is choice, possibly the greatest gift we have as human beings. We are the only known creatures at this time who have free will and choice. The blessed angels can only do God's will. We humans can choose to do it.

There is great power in the moment when decisions are made, and what matters the most is attitude. You innately know that everything is open to you, everything is still to be done and not to be done again. There is no reason for boredom on God's earth. The question you must ask yourself is, "What do I want in this life?" The first step is to be grateful that with God's grace, you always have choice.

With your natural good looks you stand out, rarely fading into the background. You have natural genius, with a mind as quick as lightning; it's delightful to hear your quips and easy-flowing rhetoric. Nevertheless it is your dilemma that you have such a hard time making decisions and often hesitate when the moment to act arrives. This causes many ups and downs, many wrong turns because of impulsive acts. It is difficult for you to recognize limitations. Consequences seem remote to you; you are not bound by laws or rules. This flexible attitude, partly wishful thinking, partly denial and a good dose of naiveté, seems to encourage a kind of magical need to seek uplifting experiences that take you out of the dreariness of daily life—which is boring to you.

It is true that thoughts bring manifestation. This gift of ingenuity isn't to be sneezed at. As an air sign you can actually materialize the future with your dreams, hopes, and wishes. Your ideas affect many people and you're responsible for that. As you've heard before I'm sure, be careful of what you wish for. As a Gemini with so much mental power you might just get it all.

In *Webster's* dictionary the word *choice* is defined as the opportunity or privilege of choosing freely. Although choice really has to do with picking or deciding, implying a critical choice, in the dictionary there is an implied positive connotation—as in *the choice* piece of food or clothing. If you look up *choice* in the thesaurus, you'll find words like *excellent, preferred, exclusive, select,* and *elegant.*

Linguistically we are encouraged to make positive selections, and who doesn't want to make the best selection possible? Choice implies either/or, but if you look deeply into the subject there are always many more subtle choices available. Take your time and see them all before jumping into the obvious. Yet, when the ego isn't integrated with the soul and the desire to control the outcome colors your choices, your decisions can be seen as self-absorbed and capricious.

The Gemini tendency to be stimulated by quick decisions, combined with an immature and inconsiderate approach, may scatter the positive effect. The natural uplifting feeling of that moment with all its natural positive energy is lost. Rational decisions are pushed aside in favor of the quick fix. It is then that selection, choices, and preferences lose their natural more positive connotations, which was not your intention at all.

June 21–July 22

Cancer in Love

ELEMENT:	Water
QUALITY:	Cardinal
PLANET:	Moon
STONE:	Pearls
COLOR:	Silver
ANIMAL:	Turtle
FLOWER:	Lily
LOVE WORDS:	Home is where the heart is

Gift — Emotional Sensitivity
Challenge — Secretiveness & Isolation

When a Cancer Falls in Love

From the day of birth, like a little sponge you absorb information from your environment.

As the moon reflects the sun with your lunar nature, mysterious and nocturnal, you reflect your surroundings just like a mirror. Your sign is instinctive, the sign of memory. From a formless state you create form. You willingly model the essence of the dynamics around your environment and the people around you. Your symbol looks like a crab, which has great meaning for Cancer. The round shape of the crab illustrates the overly sensitive nature of Cancer and the hard shell their tenacity, but if you look closely there is more there; it is two seeds in the womb, symbolizing pregnancy. As a Cancer woman you represent the highest feminine attributes and much can be learned about being a woman from watching you. As a Cancer man you are naturally endowed with the greatest of all human traits, you are a gentleman full of consideration, compassion, and grace.

We can only imagine how many times in your many lifetimes you have been in love, married, and a parent of children. Deep longings of earlier lifetimes, emotional memories, filter up through your subconscious and are subtly present in your mind from childhood throughout your life. You are born old and are highly intuitive. With so much sensitivity you naturally pick up impressions and you must learn how to work with this great gift or you could feel burdened by it.

You primary desire is to create a place of safety and comfort where you can retreat from the world. A Cancer child is the one with "the blankie" long past the age when other children abandon it. I know some Cancer children who suck their thumbs for so long it's embarrassing to themselves as well as their parents. At the same time you think like an adult and believe in some deep recess of your psyche that you must compete with grown-ups.

Ask Cancers what they need in a relationship and they'll say to build something solid, comfortable, and safe. You go for the long term. There's nothing capricious about a Cancer in love. You don't fall in love easily. The turtle and crab, creatures with hard shells that protect their soft round stomachs, symbolize your emotional sensitivity and the defenses that you set in place for protection.

Long before you could talk you were aware of subtle inner longings, and you tucked these memories away and unknowingly use them as references as an adult. These impressions may not make sense to you but your intuition takes the information and forms memories for the future. You are born consciously aware of other dimensions and the intelligence of the soul stays with you all your life. You quietly observe every detail around you until it's time to use it and are armed for life with endless impressions that flow up from the subconscious; you go out into the world a deep and soulful human being. If your childhood is disturbing the memories have a lot of fear in them and it is necessary for you to process them before you can be truly happy with yourself.

Cancerian Helen Keller's great accomplishment of overcoming the handicaps of deafness, nonspeaking, and blindness can be better understood when you realize the depth of sensitivity she had to her surroundings and appreciate the risks she took to align her limited abilities with new codes of information.

It seems as if you are passive when that couldn't be further from the truth. When something needs fixing you head right in. Cancer is a cardinal sign; a self-starter, you possess a great ambition in the world. Yet relationships remain the most important part of your life. And, as you often develop entrepreneurial skills in your late thirties, you are the sign that has the most self-made millionaires in the zodiac. Some Cancers don't "make it" until their fifties and sixties. Rightly so, I think; it's best to have something great happen to you in later life. When young you have many other avenues of enjoyment available.

You are totally open to relationships—they're number one on your list. You feel your life will be cut off if you don't have someone to love and cherish. From childhood on you have dreamed of creating a home and family. Relationships are based on intimacy and that is what you long for. It may not be easy for you but you're willing to take the time to let it develop. In relationships you are kind and affectionate. Cancers are people of principle. Rarely are you mean or callous. This may happen in the event of an extremely deprived childhood, but even then you are so nurturing that the abuse would more likely be turned back on yourself rather than against anyone else.

You will never find a Cancer dictator; that's a job for Taurus, Leo, and Capricorn. You just want to take charge of your own environment and make it grow. There is a powerful social consciousness working here. Nelson Mandela went to prison in a sacrifice for his people. Since his release he has worked unceasingly to give Africans a national role in politics. He was awarded the Nobel Prize. After Mandela got out of prison he divorced his wife; their political differences were not reconcilable and their marriage was over. Cancers often put principles above relationships. Mandela had dedicated his life to be of service to the public and could not turn a cheek to the problems his wife stirred up while he was gone. Moon-ruled Cancerians are dedicated to be of the people and are very philanthropic.

Today the sign Cancer isn't considered to be as domestic as it has in the past; many Cancerians take their organizing and nurturing skills out of the home into the business world. Cancer has become a sign of career success. A good example of this is that the United States is Cancer, born on the fourth of July. It is a country of entrepreneurs, where everyone has a chance to be successful in their chosen field. There is more wealth in the United States than in any other country in the world.

In my clientele I have found that Cancers marry more than any other sign. I always tell Cancers they'll do it until they get it right. And most often they finally do. You are very tenacious and don't give up easily.

Relating on a Soul Level

Emotional sensitivity is your gift and also your challenge.

Although you have a serious disposition, in love you throw caution to the wind. There is a strong tendency to have a poetic and romantic view of the universe. When you fall in love you are completely committed to the point of being self-sacrificing. When a relationship is working you happily put your energy into more ambitious endeavors, and that's when you reach your greatest heights.

Cancer is naturally ambitious and this can go over into your love life. Don't be naive; there is a childlike way of seeing life that must be overcome for you to pick a good partner. You want to marry someone wonderful who is suited in every way. Take your time, and allow your intuition to work. Things are not always what they seem and only an extended courtship works for you and your sensitive nature. Sadly, if the one you love spurns you, then your ambitious nature takes over and love becomes your ambition and your obsession. Your desire for love at any cost puts you in a precarious position where you give your power away and allow others the right to take unfair advantage. With your extreme loyalty it's hard to break off a negative relationship until you've tried everything. Cancer is not fainthearted.

When a man is born on this plane as a Cancer his anima (the female aspect submerged in the subconscious) is very powerful. The Dalai Lama is a Cancer. His demeanor is soft and feminine and yet he is a great ruler of his people as well as a light in the world. His unselfish teachings inspire us all. Cancerians are deeply compassionate. Although you can be moody and there is a vulnerability to hurt, your sign knows how to take action and find solutions to problems other people give up on.

Your heart's desire is to create your own power place in the world. If this is withheld for any reason you become moody and hard to get along with. It's understandable; the moon with its ebb and flow affects your bodily fluids more than other signs.

Moods are like the ocean; they change with the tide, and moodiness is the main affliction a Cancer must contend with. Out of your subconscious, feelings and emotions stew around and come up, it seems, of their own accord. By being overly sensitive to your environment you attract unrest. The test comes in how you handle this turbulence. Instead of responding completely to the changes, you must create a solid base for your own security. Take the time to get the facts and realize that you could be overreacting. You have a lot of what I call *negative imagination*. It's your choice in how you perceive the world around you; this pessimistic attitude isn't necessary. Here is a list of questions you might ask yourself as a check point on moodiness.

1. Am I letting past disappointments ruin my chances for a productive and joy-filled life?

2. Am I seeing the world the way it should be and not as it really is?

3. Am I setting my mind on hopeless goals instead of what is really available to me?

4. Do I choose to worry when life is offering me my dreams?

5. Do I live in the past because the present forces me to make choices?

6. Do I victimize yourself by having to be right all the time?

When you are in love with someone and letting the relationship take the time it needs to evolve, it pays off. On the other hand, being so emotionally sensitive, with a tendency to be a perfectionist, you can be filled with fear and self-doubt. You like to achieve; mistakes are forbidden. Trying to prove yourself is draining and keeps you from the joy of just living your life. Because of your sensitive nature it takes you a long time to accept love, but when you do it is lasting. Cancer is a sign of great endurance and tenacity. After becoming exclusive it takes a lot to make you give up on a relationship. Your natural tendency is to encourage things to grow. You are best when you adhere to the principle of gradual development with all that entails.

In a way there is no such thing as failure. There are good and bad times in our lives certainly, and bad things happen to good people all the time. However, the bad times are when we learn the most. When things don't turn out as we expected, hard as it is to swallow, it's the time that you can be awakened to the real world, and create the clarity of vision known to those who have risked and have tasted disappointments. These disappointments, or failures you might call them, are just one part of a life for those who dare to live fully. If there are no ups and downs the fabric of your life is very thin. Avoiding risks takes you into the isolated part of yourself, where self-pity is in control. That is not who you are! Sadly, if you choose this direction you never learn how to enjoy yourself until later, after the midlife crisis. That's when you are more likely to lighten up and decide not to take life so seriously. You realize that life is meant to be joyous. It's an opportunity to integrate your mind and feelings and create a loving space for all you love.

Blocking Yourself from Love

You are so private that you could be called covert.

A part of you wants to hide out in a secret place. As much as you love your partner you can still shut down and disappear. Deep inside every Cancer is a place that no one else can find, where you allow yourself to shut down and cease communication. When you feel threatened for whatever reason, you allow irrational fears and confusion to take over. Your poor partner is totally abandoned when you go there. They feel rejected for something they haven't done and it is damaging to the relationship.

You must learn to stop this destructive behavior. You deserve privacy; we all do, but you can at least give your partner warning of your need to process thoughts and feelings.

Perhaps your partner can be with you in this quiet time. Whatever you decide it has to be with love and consideration. By allowing new forms of communication to develop you can create an intimacy that works for you both.

Cancer is a survival sign, much like Taurus; there seems to be an underlying fear that brings you daily unrest. This free-floating fear doesn't really have a name. It can fit most situations; with a bad attitude, moody Cancer can scan any situation and find something wrong. "There's always a fly in the ointment," my mother used to say, and it's true. You can always find something wrong, but on the other hand you can also find what is good. Most situations have both. So don't forget to look for the good as well or your life becomes a narrow road of fear, anxiety, and hostility.

You long for constancy, yet the Moon as your ruler indicates that what is constant in your life is change. You are very responsive to the phases of the Moon. With life's changing scene you are able to delve deeply into your essential nature, and from this depth comes clarity.

Your mother is the most important figure in your life bar none and there is always an issue of some kind with her even if your early childhood was ideal. No one ever really overcomes his mother's influence, and least of all you Cancers. The perception of an all-powerful mother and dependent child creates a dynamic Cancers act out in relationships until they mature past this drama of extremes. In fact, Cancer is the sign that rules the family and particularly the mother.

Paradoxically (and you may want to deny it), either you marry someone like your mother or you become like her. With the perfectionist tendencies so evident in the cardinal signs, and the pressure that comes from that, you want security and you run the gamut of a childish need to be parented or wanting to parent your partner. This is out of balance; relationships work best when two adults come together. Granted some adult parenting can be healthy, we all need nurturing. It's when there's a wound from childhood and one of the partners is needy that it gets out of balance. Some Cancerians act out emotionally until they've created a trail of pain for themselves as well as others.

A codependent parent/child coupling is incestuous and doomed. This is what I call taking on wounded birds. Women are a guilty as men in this dilemma.

A Cancer woman wants to marry someone who is stronger. Being so strong yourself, this kind of partner is hard to find. You are a great actress, playing the role of being helpless by calling your husband ten times a day and checking on him; or conversely, you can take charge of the household, finances and all, even the roles that are usually considered to be the male partner's. Without a good role model to help you, maturing is a difficult process.

As a Cancer man you know that women are all-powerful: you were probably raised in a mother-dominated world. If the mother isn't present, there is always a grandmother or an aunt to take her place. You were either too close to your mother symbol, seeking her approval, or you were afraid of her and wanted to get away. All the women in your life take on her qualities. If you project the mother role onto your partner your relationship is over from the start.

I don't want to sound like a mother basher, I am far from it. I'm a mother myself. Yet Cancer is extremely sensitive to family matters. The process of growing past childhood into adulthood is especially painful for Cancer. Remember, you were born with a neutral awareness that absorbed everything around you, but without the maturity to sort it out. You have to live awhile to thread this useful information through your life. The worst can always happen, I suppose; there is always a chance of failure, although I believe the universe wants to bring us what we need. Give hope a chance!

A Cancer Love Story

This is a story about a Cancer man and how he has learned to communicate his needs and wants to his wife and children.

This story starts with the sister. I was reading her chart and she asked about her brother. I saw in her chart that he was very tied to his mother, and when I asked what sign, I knew even more. He was a Cancer and it's their nature to feel responsible for the mother. He even worked in his father's business. In case you don't know this, an astrologer can see everyone that is of importance in your natal chart. There is a house in the chart for parents, mates, children, the work you're suited for, and even what kind of neighbors you would have in your environment.

Their parents were divorced when they were teenagers. Since then the brother had graduated from college and married, but he still couldn't break his emotional tie with his mother. He spent a good deal of time with her, leaving his family at home.

I told the sister to tell him that he was going to have to handle the situation or he would become depressed and his own family would suffer.

The next day I had a phone call. He wanted an appointment. He was ready to hear what his chart had to tell him.

When I read his chart I realized he was ready to move forward, he just didn't know what to do. He needed to look at himself as an adult person who had needs of his own. Close family relationships are great but not when they move into dependency and block you from growing in your own relationships.

His marriage had the possibility of becoming soul bonded but he didn't know how to put his wife first. In some ways he and his wife were still in the courtship and early commitment phases of a relationship (even though they already had children!). He had stopped growing emotionally as a teenager and although he was highly intelligent he didn't have a sense of identity of his own. Both husband and wife are in therapy. They still live close to Mom but there are boundaries set and now his own family comes first. He is no longer guilt ridden and emotionally dependent. He can become the wonderful husband and father he wants to be.

Your Most Authentic Self

Cancer is the fourth house in the zodiac and is the first sign to enter the passive side of the chart that defines one's relationship to others.

The six signs on the left of the zodiac circle are independent. As I have discussed earlier, the first relationship of emotional dependence starts with the mother. You have a need to be needed.

One fact about Cancer that is often overlooked is that Cancer rules trade, business, and the ocean, where maritime trade was carried out. Cancers are great business people and are the self-made millionaires of the zodiac. They like to hold on to money, and many Cancerians collect property and other things of value that grow in value. Often they become wealthy in their later years.

You are your best when you are in love. The unstable emotional longings settle down and you feel that your life has meaning. The key for Cancer is to not take so much responsibility for family. You are naturally generous with your affection but you need nurturing too. Your lesson in life is to receive love and not always be the one to give so much. Opening up to your inner child in a healthy way is very important to you. You are young in heart and you have much to share.

July 23–August 22

Leo in Love

ELEMENT:	Fire
QUALITY:	Fixed
PLANET:	Sun
STONE:	Amber
COLOR:	Gold
ANIMAL:	Lion
FLOWER:	Sunflower
LOVE WORDS:	Baby! Baby! Baby!

Gift — A Loving Heart
Challenge — Self-Centeredness

When a Leo Falls in Love

Leos are the eternal children of the zodiac.

Love is your favorite thing. If you're not in a relationship you are looking high and low for just the right one and you're rarely alone very long. When you fall in love it's like Christmas and you're the star on top of the tree. Not only do you want to be cherished, you want to love someone, too, and in your typical unstinting fashion you shower your loved one with affection and gifts. You like to be adored and with God's blessing you are easy to love.

You are famous for your generosity. You know that the universe is abundant and have no doubt that you are worthy of all its bounty. With confidence in your continuing ability to attract more and more you are never stingy. Nevertheless, as far as a Leo is concerned there is a feeling of ownership involved in giving. You will give to the ends of the earth to someone you love, but you have to grow into philanthropy. To send money out into the unknown isn't your favorite activity. You generously give your mate expensive jewelry knowing it's as much for your pleasure as it is for hers. Even though you are known as a gambler it's the game that you're committed to; your positive outlook won't let you even think of losing.

Lucky you, you are ruled by the Sun—the driving force behind our beautiful solar system. And Leos do shine. You are the bright and shining star of the zodiac and you stand out wherever you are with a strong presence and dramatic good looks. Your appearance is always notable and even if not classically beautiful you have the charm and good-humored presence that attracts people to you.

It is with great bearing and tremendous vitality that you pull a circle of people together, then take command like a great king, queen, or general. With your strong personality people listen to you and look to you for guidance—maybe partly because you have a great delivery. With a natural sense of theater and a melodious iambic pentameter you sound as if you know what you're saying. Maybe Shakespeare (although he was a Taurus) had some Leo in his chart! Movie magnates Cecil B. DeMille, Samuel Goldwyn, and John Huston, all Leos, were award-winning movie makers in California, a Leo state. Many Leos are actors, as are a lot of politicians, which probably adds up to the same thing. You'll find very few Leos that like to have a desk job. They want to be where the action is and life usually takes them there.

Sometimes a Leo goes all the way into the outrageous. Artist and film producer Andy Warhol decided that he would be a celebrity, and had more than his fifteen minutes of fame, as his art is still at the top of art collectors' lists. Leos do have staying power.

Even though Leo is the lover of the zodiac, you like your own space. You're the ruler of the cat family and cats need comfort and a feeling of control in their environment. There is a Leo I know that has his own TV room downstairs; the one for the family is upstairs. This need for a controlled environment isn't about being antisocial; it just that being on-stage constantly is a little draining and Leos need to be renewed for the next big scene.

Another Leo who was over the top with big ideas was Napoleon. His ambition took him from life as a lowly soldier all the way to emperor. In a typical Leo penchant for the dramatic he even crowned himself! He didn't deem anyone high enough in the land to put the crown on his head. That's a grand attitude for you. Of course his hubris found him and brought him down in Russia, a country ruled by Aquarius, his polar opposite sign. There is a lesson in that: we must honor our opposite sign, where the healing of our ego is. Balance will come to us all in one way or the other.

When you make a commitment, you take it very seriously. Leo and Libra have a lot in common in that they are signs of courtship and marriage. Leo rules the courtship part of a relationship, while the Libra rules the legal commitment, when you say "I do." Leo is heartfelt and Libra follows the laws of society. Like Libra you lean toward observing the proprieties. You like to live within the expectations of what is considered socially acceptable. Royalty with all its pomp and ritual is a Leo manifestation. The royal family of England doesn't like to change their archaic and seemingly antiquated etiquette. Sometimes it takes tragedy, as in the death of rebellious Princess Diana (who had an Aquarius moon), to revamp rigid and outdated customs and to make way for new and progressive protocol.

Your Nature Is Fiery and Affectionate

The element of fire refers to a universal radiance that is excitable, enthusiastic, and colorful.

You have a natural radiance that affects the people around you. You are responsible for your effect and it is absolutely necessary for you to set your intention on high spiritual understanding. The feeling function gives you awareness of the emotions of pleasure or displeasure. These feelings are evoked by what you perceive and how you allow these events to affect your behavior are, of course, your choice. As a fixed sign, along with Taurus, Scorpio, and Aquarius, you are gifted in focus. Your actions are fabulous when your intentions are good. Intention and focus create the world. It may be easy for you to know what you want, but how does it affect others? This is an area where you may fall short. An intention is not only a desire; it is the use of your will, and as a Leo yours is particularly dynamic. If you make up your mind to have something or someone, you probably will. If you close your mind that's that.

As a Leo you don't want to hurt other people. You respect the rights of others. Your mistakes are never from bad intentions. The faults of fire sign feelers, particularly Leo, have to do with not being sensitive to others' needs. Knowing how to take care of yourself very well, you project that power onto others and can't understand at all when they don't live up to your expectations. Don't project your fiery nature onto others. There are some who are not so brave or strong as you.

We think of the earth as dirt and stone, but deep in the earth the core is pure fire. It is your right to pull that fire up from the earth into your heart. Let it come through you and inspire others. As a fire sign you understand innately how to do this. The lion rules the instinctual animal nature, that is your gift in life and with your lion heart you become more conscious, more open-minded, and consequentially you make a great leader. Mistakes are made, sure, then you do what it takes to make things right and learn from it.

Relating on a Soul Level

There are realms of gold hidden in the depth of our hearts, according to an old Hindu proverb.

Singularly the most consequential fact about the sign Leo is that it rules the heart, which is symbolic of the love principle. The heart is the center of the body where the upper and the lower chakras meet. When you want something that is important, you often hold your hand over your heart for emphasis. It has been said that the earth is the heart chakra of a great being, which is composed of the solar system. As earthlings we all are connected to this cosmic fire.

I have read that the sound of the great *om* from India, which turned into *amen* in the west, is the key to God consciousness. It is the sound of earth and it is drawn as a circle with a dot—the symbol for the Sun. This symbol represents the soul. With the Sun as your ruler you are connected with the sound of the soul. As a being of light, with every breath, you form your life.

All great religions talk about the heart. When you feel right within your heart you can do great things. There is a warm fire inside that imparts a joyous nature. It has been said many times by many great poets and writers that the heart holds the power and the purpose of who you are.

You want to love with all your heart. As the sign of the Sun you naturally give out light; you illuminate the material world around you with your glow. When you are with the one you love you have the ability to recharge your environment with vital power, and all who are lucky to be around you are blessed by this transcendent radiance. To come to terms with the fact that light makes shade, you mustn't be fearful of the dark; it's a part of the light. To be soul-conscious and open your heart to what's the highest and best puts you in a vulnerable position. You will be tested. That is part of being children of the Sun.

Joseph Campbell writes extensively about the hero in his book *Hero with a Thousand Faces*. The fatality of heroism is the need to overcome the enemy. This is the eternal drama of light and life—of power and of love overcoming evil. In an individuation process that Jung talks about, there is a battle with the ego and the self (the soul). There is a crisis point in a Leo's life, where you Leos are forced to face your inner nature. It feels like you are actually dying. The death is really a conflict between the two opposites, the yes side and the no side of life, which are always in conflict. Leos don't like to say no, so it is always there underneath pulling on them and trying to throw them off balance.

After some time of reflection you emerge a more neutral (this is good) human being, more compassionate. Your emotional nature becomes the servant instead of the king and there is an opening to a deeper more fulfilling talent of compassionately serving others. This battle of the opposites brings in the power of your opposite sign, Aquarius, who is the humanitarian. Our opposite sign always has the answer to our quest for balance.

Being a fire sign you are enthusiastic and demonstrative by nature. In your optimistic way you believe that it is your divine right to create something wonderful. The only drawback here is that your point of view is often childish, egocentric, and idealistic. You may be overdeveloped in your feeling of entitlement and with open-hearted idealism rush in where even angels fear to tread.

You must learn humility. When you buy into your own self-importance and the illusion that you are in control, you are out of balance with the flow of life. This way of thinking creates chaos and consequently failure. (Think of Napoleon.)

Egocentric decisions dissipate your ability to win your objective. A Leo must live his life in such a way that he can have fulfilling dreams. Humility is the virtue that allows you to see the balancing force in each situation.

Blocking Yourself from Love

Your challenge of being self-centered is what puts pressure on your relationships.

Leos are by nature superstars. It's hard to keep the momentum going. Sooner or later you must share your hopes, wishes, fears, and sorrows with someone else. To keep up a good front you can end up acting your life instead of being a normal human being. Have you ever noticed how many Hollywood actors end up in the hospital with exhaustion?

Your desire is to create a great moment but there is no real understanding of how to be intimate with your partner. You have a tendency to push hard for what you want and not consider your partner's real needs. The heat from the Sun can be extreme. Mere mortals have a hard time getting close to you. You are a consummate actor—your loved ones may never know your real feelings or thoughts. How can they if you don't know them yourself? There is a tendency to lump all feeling into either black or white, good or bad, the yes or no battle. It's hard for you to see the grays; the subtleties are lost in the heat of the Sun. In your need for attention, praise, and recognition, you can bypass the joy of an intimate relationship.

Leos need to take pause, think through what they're doing, and get feedback. Let's not forget you are the lover of the zodiac; you're not above sweet talk. Let your partner know the power he has over you to make you happy. Ask your partner what he needs to be happy with you. It takes a strong person to stand up to you, and you must respect that person for loving you enough to call you on your stuff. You project what you want onto others, then you are surprised when they rebel against you.

Female Leos are always masculine in their approach to life. They like to be the dynamic ones and can dominate a relationship. It's the male lion that is the symbol for Leo, not the female. Just look at a pride of lions; it's the female that does all the work. The male lion is lounging around; he likes total allegiance and the choice piece of the kill.

I found this poem in my files. A client sent it to me. Although it's good material for any Sun sign, I think Leos could benefit from tacking this up on their bulletin boards.

Letting Go

To let go is not to care for,
but to care about.

To let go is not to fix,
but to be supportive.

To let go is not to judge,
but to allow another to be a human being.

To let go is not to be protective,
it is to permit another to face reality.

To let go is to admit powerlessness,
which means the outcome is not in my hands.

To let go is not to regret the past,
but to grow and live for the future.

To let go is to fear less and love more.

You are a mover and shaker, you always play an important part of every situation you come into. All eyes are on you, kid! To let go of your unapproachable manner takes great courage. But risking forces you to develop trust.

When asked about his interest in Tibetan Buddhism, Richard Gere said, "When you're on a spiritual path, your heart expands and touches everyone around you. And when you're not on a spiritual path, your heart is restricted, and touches everyone around you." With an open mind and an open heart you can change the world. You are here to learn the lessons of humility and adaptability. Your big heart and intense loyalty helps to strike a partnership between your keen mental awareness and your natural instinct for love.

The initiation you must go through is to simplify your life. To stay lit up in endless drama is impossible. As every day has a nighttime, every relationship has dark moments. With truth and surrender to the heart your path becomes light. What must be surrendered is the desire of the ego to remain separate and in control. You are never in control anyway; that is the illusion of the human condition. There are myriad things going on at many different levels. Much more is happening than you could ever guess. The surprise element of the universe is what gives us freedom to grow.

Love Is King

Leos can charm the birds right out of the trees, but is charm enough?

There's a great line in a Sondheim musical *Into the Woods*, a story based on the old fairy tales. In the first act the goose laid the golden egg, Cinderella married the Prince, everything turned out just like the old stories say. It was in the second act after the happy ending that the story changed. It was what happened after the fairy tale came true. After Cinderella and the Prince were married and had a child, Prince Charming was caught red-handed having an affair. To a teary Cinderella, the Prince nonchalantly said, "I was taught to be charming, not sincere."

This seems to be a classic love story for Leos until they are able to mature past the golden child syndrome. For you, romance and excitement is everything. When you are in a relationship it becomes a drama. What starts out as a romance soon becomes strained by too much sexual tension and great expectations. It's not easy to keep such an intense love affair going. When the relationship reaches a fever pitch it starts to crack at the seams.

You might think that as a Leo the wisdom of having a successful relationship is inborn. It's not. As far as love is concerned, the distinction between your perception and reality gets a bit blurry. You might not know it, but there was no such thing as romance for the average person until the seventeenth century. The words that describe romance in the dictionary are *legend, heroic, adventure, mysterious, imaginary,* and *supernatural.* To romance someone, the dictionary suggests, is to exaggerate or invent detail or incident.

The word *roman* comes from Rome, a Leo country, as is France, where the first romantic novels were written. This information is not written in disdain, but rather to show the illusions of love that you put on a pedestal when you first enter a love affair. Most romances don't end up well. Think of the tragic end in *Romeo and Juliet,* and the story of Cinderella may not have turned out as well as you thought. Many times Leos get stuck in the romantic stage. With all the books written about love and romance you'd think we'd all be better at moving past the fantasy stage and moving into true love.

Leos love the idea of chemistry and magic. The elements of expectation, anticipation, and romance are often far more important than the actual physical act of love. You love the feeling that this is the first time that anyone ever felt this way and that's where you get stuck. Your heart is true but it is true to an ideal rather than to an individual.

A good romance is one that is grounded. Your sign loves

courtship and if you are patient you can develop a romance that is satisfying to both of you. It is not a matter of just finding the right person but of developing an attraction into a mature love. Since Leo rules the falling in love part of courtship, you might get stuck on the turntable of falling in love again and again and again. The question for a Leo is how to move past the romance (Leo) into reality (Virgo) and into commitment (Libra) with comfort. Lighten up, don't take your love life so personally. Let go of the outcome and enjoy the moment. As long as lovers maintain an idealized, incomplete view of each other, they live in a confining imaginary world.

Learn from your opposite sign Aquarius that friendship needs to be included. A mature love is more fulfilling than a fantasy, Leo. It just takes a different perspective. Try it out, you'll see.

Your Most Authentic Self

Leos can really get along with everyone if they decide to.

You like a lot of feedback. A person who can stand up to you and meet you on equal footing keeps you interested and creates a matrix for true satisfaction. But woe be it to anyone who tries to change you or control you.

As a Leo you stand out. You emulate a bold and confident manner. Leo likes to be grand, and even when you go into battle your flags are flying and the band is playing. You are easy to read; there are generally no secrets here, and if there are supposed to be, you tell on yourself. Just like a child, it's hard for you to keep a secret.

Your greatest failing is pride, yet your greatest asset is self-confidence. How to keep this balanced is what your life is about. If a situation needs accessing you are the best. You are able to extract the heart of a situation and make it manifest.

This is a great challenge but one that is complementary to your nature, to sum up the situation in a complete way like a great lawyer in his summation at the end of the trial.

When a Leo outgrows self-importance and forgoes emotion, for logic, he is capable of great things. By understanding the potential of an opportune moment, no matter what the idea is, as a Leo, you have the ability to capture something extraordinary and do something great with it. But you have to stay on your toes. You never know when you'll have an opportunity to have a great moment. Of all the signs, you are the most capable to capturing the momentum and running with it.

Your love life is one of your great moments. As you learn to let go of the fantasy that your mate has the power to make you whole and start to grow in consciousness, there is hope of creating a sense of wholeness together. You can

- Create a more accurate picture of your partner.

- Communicate your needs and desires to your partner.

- Value your partner's needs and desires as much as your own.

- No longer deny the darker side of your personality.

- Allow your partner to teach you what he or she knows.

- Learn how to grow in commitment with courage and discipline.

It is only when you see love as an opportunity that you can enter into a true romance. Love is the fire that lights the way to marriage and commitment. When we realize that relationships are vehicles for change and self-growth then we can begin to satisfy our unconscious yearnings for a perfect love.

August 23–September 22

Virgo in Love

ELEMENT:	Earth
QUALITY:	Mutable
PLANET:	Mercury
STONE:	Sapphire
COLOR:	Pale Green
ANIMALS:	Cats and dogs
FLOWER:	Buttercup
LOVE WORDS:	How do I love thee? Let me count the ways.

Gift — Discernment
Challenge — Ambivalence

When a Virgo Falls in Love

Let's get rid of the old myth that Virgos are virgins or monks and do not want to have a relationship.

It is true that you are a very discriminating person, but you are also an earth sign and have all the sensual yearnings of your fellow earth signs, Capricorn and Taurus. Earth signs like tangible feedback, and a loving relationship is at the top of the list. One of the major needs of humans is to love and be loved back. It's as important as water and air. It may take a lot to melt your heart, but when you find yourself in love's crucible you are aflame with love and take a long time to cool down. The reputation of being celibate comes from the fact that you are so discerning that you will wait to meet the right one, plus the fact that you are very hard to please. Virgos have difficulty expressing their desires. You have inquiring minds and excellent memories. You always seem to be asking how, why, when, and where. You may seem totally self-sufficient, but you are happier when you have someone to love, who loves you back.

You are very civilized and it's important to you how things look and whether everything is in order. If you want good food and wine ask a Virgo where to eat, or better still go to her house for dinner. Even Virgo men can put an excellent meal together. Your refrigerators are full of delectable tidbits that no one else takes the time to seek out. If you're a health nut so much the better. You know how to make health food taste good.

Health, diet, and digestion are of great concern to Virgo. Virgo rules the colon. It's part of a monitoring system in the body and there is an internal wisdom that knows what is good for the body and what it needs to eliminate. Elimination is a great power—without it we would be walking garbage cans, mentally, emotionally, and physically. Yet your gift of discernment can be carried too far and your critical nature can be upsetting to your partner. In your mental way it's hard for you to let go of the analyzing head talk and just enjoy being with your loved one.

The truth is you're more comfortable by yourself. There is always a sense of isolation in Virgo, a deep-seated love of privacy. You like be detached in order to sort things out, but at the same time you can feel deeply lonely and left out. There is always work to do. It's like the old saying, "Women's work is never done"; a Virgo is always editing and rearranging. Deep inside of you there is an uncontrollable urge to clean up, clean out, and start again. Virgo is a sign of change and process. You must be careful of your love of editing, because you can be too stringent and coldly discard more than you need to. Minimal is good but austerity is for priests and monks. Really!

When you clean house you don't throw away the dishes or the furniture; it's the same with a relationship. The irony is that you crave attachment. You want to be freed from your prison of loneliness, and yet at the same time you ferociously hunger for freedom, and yes, neatness. By constantly being in the objective position trying to see what's wrong you remove yourself emotionally from the one you love.

The solution can be found in your opposite sign, Pisces. Pisces is soft and yielding. A sign of great understanding, forgiveness, and compassion, all traits that are suppressed in you and need integration. It is within your reach to know your partner's needs and create an intimacy that heals your self-induced loneliness. When you move into a state of trust, the boundaries are more subtle and there is more spontaneity in your relationship. You are a planner and strategist so you will never jump in without a lot of reflection. This is your gift—don't let it be your curse.

Your Nature Is Earthy and Productive

As an earth sign you only trust what can be discerned by the senses.

"What you see is what you get" is an earth sign's slogan. Earth sign sensors rely more on practical reason than on theories or inspiration, and on the plus side you have more natural patience and self-discipline than the thinking (air), feeling (fire), and intuiting (water) types of personalities. You are cautious, somewhat conventional, very dependable, and take care of yourself very well, even in times of great stress. There is a deep need to straighten everything out, clean it up, and make it work, but that is much too clinical for other types of personalities.

Professor Higgins in *My Fair Lady* must be a Virgo and an

earth sign sensor. As he sings "Why Can't a Woman Be More Like a Man?" he admonishes Liza Doolittle "to clean up the mess inside." She has to be a Pisces.

Earth sign men (especially Virgos) with a penchant for parenting often marry wounded birds, people whose lives have been hard and who are unsure of themselves, and set out to improve them. It never works and their partners leave them after they've become bored with being parented. They already have parents that caused the problem in the first place.

Virgo women are often good daughters—following their families' dictates that they find someone who has a good job, is dependable, or just marry the most suitable person that's around at the time. Many times they meet someone else that is more suited to them at a later date and there is a lot of heartbreak.

The movie *Elizabeth* was a good example of a Virgo's dilemma. When she was young and carefree she fell in love with Lord Dudley. How wonderful he was—a good friend, charming, so passionately in love with her, he said, yet he was the first to betray her. The political climate in England at that time was such that Elizabeth had to be totally focused or great upheaval would descend on her country, so she married England. That's not out of the ordinary for a Virgo; many of them marry their jobs. England is lucky she was a Virgo.

Virgos of today seem to make similar decisions. You can be a victim of too much duty and discipline, self-control and methodical routines. Lighten up. You can achieve your goals and give a relationship the time it needs to grow. Of course that is the answer—*the time it needs to grow*. And also perhaps the benefit of the doubt.

Relating on a Soul Level

Oscar Wilde said, "There is nothing that will cure the senses but the soul, and nothing that will cure the soul but the senses."

Virgo is a feminine sign, and as a Virgo, either male or female, you have the traits necessary to accomplish great things. The feminine energy is the producer in life. Virgo is the sign that rules form. There is no task too detailed or complex for you and your agile mind. Although masculine energy is usually considered to be mental, in Virgo you find that the feminine as well as the masculine signs have logic and mental fortitude.

Virgo rules production. After every action there is a process and you Virgos are good at making things work, especially when you look at what's best for all.

As a Virgo you want your relationship to be chosen in a practical fashion; there's no second-guessing here. Remember the heart is where your challenge of discernment lies. Not many people can pass your close scrutiny. When you are centered with an open heart and at peace with the process of courtship everything falls into place and you will find the one who's right for you.

Blocking Yourself from Love

As a Virgo you are adept in the world of form—with an innate eye for detail, perspective, structure, and just making things work.

You are an example of the old chestnut that *you can't see the forest for the trees* when your focus is on the small and mostly unimportant things. He wears the wrong clothes, or she doesn't have the right degree. It doesn't matter what, there is always something. Your critical eye goes to a problem and gets stuck right there. That is until you grow out of your tendency to see what's wrong and ignore what's right. Your partner would like some good words occasionally.

You can get very pedantic and even boring. Virgo is sometimes called the starched mother or even the critical mother, because there is such a tendency to analyze, categorize, and put everything in its place that you lose sight of enjoyment. This emotionally dry thinking is why you are continually searching and evaluating. Then you're back to the frog pond again, kicking around feeling isolated and alone.

A Virgo Love Story

Long ago when the goddess ruled supreme the symbol for Virgo was the beautiful goddess Isis, holding a baby and a sheath of grain.

The symbols of the zodiac are so beautiful, they not only give us insight into ancient history, they also contain clues into the spiritual knowledge of ancient times.

Isis is not the all-powerful great goddesses symbol. She is instead a much softer feminine icon, an intermediary between God and man. She plays the role of the messenger, drawing her power off of her father, the great Thoth, another Virgo. Thoth was the scribe of the sun god Ra. He wrote all the ancient treatises on magic and astrology. Isis studied with her father for years and developed her skills before she went into the world with her mission. She is similar to the women of today, who wait until later to marry. She learned all her father had to teach her and brought the secrets of the gods to mankind in order for them to be healed and assured of immortality. An important part of Isis as the symbol for Virgo is that she is holding a child. This is an archetypal symbol of the

Madonna and child, which shows up for the first time in Egyptian mythology and later in Christianity. Both virgins, Isis and Mary had immaculate conceptions. This doesn't sound so far-fetched anymore. With all the new technology in the twenty-first century many women will have a chance to have children later in life without being impregnated by a man.

The grain is a symbol of horticulture and honors the unknown ancient people who developed cultivated crops as we know them. Grain is a symbol of fertility and commemorates the harvest, which was celebrated in the Virgo time, when the grains were harvested in Egypt. It is a humble symbol of abundance as reflected in the Lord's Prayer, "Give us this day our daily bread."

Isis studies and waits; she has great patience. She responds well and efficiently in crisis. Waiting and doing her duty are very characteristic of Virgo. In a relationship, a Virgo fares better when she waits until later to pick a mate. You Virgos often do not connect with your feeling function until you have learned a skill and have patiently put it into practice.

The love story of Isis and Osiris is one of the most passionate and devoted love stories in recorded history. Isis was an exquisite example of Virgo. Everywhere she went, she took her teaching and healing skills. She was the good wife and nurturing mother, as well as a horticulturist and midwife. She could heal the sick. Even though she was a queen she had great humility and served the needs of her people. Her story makes one think of Mother Teresa, who was also a Virgo. Although Mother Teresa was married to the church, it was still a marriage.

Osiris and Isis are great archetypes of the male and female. Osiris was a sun god and Isis was a lunar goddess of discrimination and excellence. Without Isis, Osiris was immobilized. It is a story very similar to Shiva and Shakti, the Hindu gods that illustrate the perfect balance of male and female energy, where the feminine acts out the power of the male energy.

I know a Virgo who had wanted to get married so badly it kept her upset all the time. She felt that her life was slipping away and she could never have what she wanted. The problem was that her job kept her traveling constantly. Few people want a part-time relationship—and neither did she. Her heart yearned to be with someone. She had all the traits of a wonderful partner. Although she was very discriminating in her nature, she was very understanding at the same time—there was no reason for her not to find a mate. The problem here was that her priorities were off; she never put love first. She went home for a high school reunion, connected with someone that she had been in school with but had known only slightly, and within six weeks' time she was married.

I have seen this happen to many Virgos: after looking for a long time there is a tendency to give up, then meet someone and marry quickly. It's a big risk. Pushing good sense aside, you make up your mind and that's that.

Beware of quick marriages. Hurrying so nothing can go wrong is a big risk. I think that marriage is an important decision and time is needed to really know your partner. Our Virgo friend made her marriage work. It was her choice to begin a marriage without much prior information; there are no wrong choices, only consequences. Perhaps this was the only time in her life that she allowed her heart to open no matter how great the risk of being hurt. The attraction was there and there was enough compatibility to grow together. It wasn't easy.

Going back and forth in emotional matters is very draining and there is no hope of resolution until you let go of the part of yourself that resists joy. As a Virgo you can't deny this pessimistic tendency. Truth works for everyone. Don't be afraid to let your partner know how you feel. Healing is a process, not an event. Be patient and persevere.

Serious talking is necessary to grow together. Here are three questions you can ask yourself when things get rough:

1. What is not being said?

2. What is not being heard?

3. What is not being noticed?

Love is always a risk. Why do you think we say "fall in love"? We can't just think ourselves in love; courtship is an emotional process. It takes two strangers who through some magic happening become close and agree to live their lives together. You don't find many partners who are suitable, but sooner or later, especially if you continue to grow and mature, a wonderful person will be there for you to share your life with.

There are social customs in most countries that help you through the dating process, but in the new age these props are falling away, forcing each person to learn how to grow together in his and her own way. Today when you enter into a relationship you're pretty much on your own as far as society is concerned. The Virgo stage of courtship is the beginning of real communication and trust.

Your Most Authentic Self

When Virgos learn how to accept grace into their lives there is an immediate change for the better.

Wherever Virgo appears in a natal chart there is always an element of service, and because of your opposite sign, Pisces, there is sacrifice. Virgo is the phase of discrimination that takes you to marriage and commitment in Libra. It's the back-off stage in the process of soul bonding. As you turn the corner of the seventh house and go into the Libra, the focus changes to being aware of others' needs. As a Virgo it's important for you to be aware of what you need and want in a partner before you can take someone into your heart. Virgo as a mutable sign is very adaptable. You offer a relationship flexibility that enables individuality. But be careful, if all you will offer is correct form, the result could be a heartless romance, and love will fly out the window.

Virgos want love and affection like everybody else. Yet you are uncomfortable with it. Love has to do with feelings and emotions and you have put those aside in early life, trying to do things correctly. Virgos are generally very attractive and pull in relationships easily. Yes, you do meet people, you do fall in love and have a chance to be happy in a relationship. In fact, being so wise you often know your heart from the very beginning. The problem you have is that it takes a challenge or extreme excitement to make you let down your barriers. In an attempt to protect yourself, you become too critical. Virgos are very busy people. You like to take on projects that are full of detail and immensely time consuming. You are much more comfortable with work, problem solving, and solutions, not romantic fantasy. When your emotions arise (and they do) you find yourself fragmented and confused. On the positive side, with your observant ways, if a relationship has problems it doesn't take you very long until you let your partner know what you think. Recognizing the problem areas helps you to work on a solution. Remember that life is a mirror. It always reflects back what you need to know about yourself. If you continue to attract people who aren't right for you, you need to take a long look at yourself.

You are highly intuitive and very close to nature. Virgo rules plants, herbs, and small domestic animals. Your own natural body, connected to all the orders of living things, is wiser, sharper, and quicker on the uptake than your civilized self. Let nature carry you. Thinking too much severs links with guidance of the heart. Your intuitive body will support you unerringly if you don't interfere or try to control it. You don't have to be stuck in the mind, that comes from childhood fears. Express yourself naturally, emanate instinct and impulse. Let the chips fall where they may.

The key is to hold both your partner and yourself in high esteem. You can learn something from Leos, who feel naturally that they deserve the best. When you find a balance point do not be swayed by sentiment and do things that will not serve both parties well. Take your time, listen, contemplate the facts, and state the truth; then you will be able to enjoy intimacy and commitment.

September 23–October 22

Libra in Love

ELEMENT:	Air
QUALITY:	Cardinal
PLANET:	Venus
STONE:	Opal
COLORS:	Pale blue and green
ANIMAL:	Turtledove
FLOWER:	Hydrangea
LOVE WORDS:	I do!

Gift — Cooperation
Challenge — Romantic Fantasy & Vacillation

When a Libra Falls in Love

When you love someone, that person is lucky indeed, for there is no one who could be more attentive and solicitous than you.

Your planetary ruler is Venus, the planet of love, devotion, affection, and passion. Venus makes things easy and enjoyable. She is comfortable with nature, a feminine form of strength. She gives you permission to ask for and receive what you need. Blessed by Venus, cooperation is your natural state and you will stretch yourself to the limit to stay neutral when in a stressful situation. Your sense of fairness and your steady foundation helps you make the most loving decisions that are possible.

You abhor unpleasant things and avoid confrontation when you can. Yet there is a dichotomy here; by being so positive you give the impression of being unaware of what's going on around you. Nothing could be further from the truth. Your mind is like a laser with such piercing insight that you never miss a thing.

People matter more to you than facts and data. Your nature is patient and kind; you would do anything not to make waves. It's live and let live in your life. Librans seem to have a deep inner knowing that there is a divine plan in life and that it unfolds moment by moment.

Myths tell us that Venus was born unsullied from the sky god Uranus's genitals. Saturn, Uranus's vengeful son, castrated his father and dropped his genitals into the sea where they spawned the beautiful Venus. We've all seen at least a replica of the *Birth of Venus*, by Italian Renaissance painter Botticelli. Both of her parents were formless, so Venus has no real physical model here on earth. Her form is ideal and her perfect features show a symmetry nonpareil. Without the element of time, which Saturn rules, we wouldn't have our beautiful love goddess. Uranus, who lives in cosmic time concepts that we earthlings can only hope to comprehend, gave earthlings a gift of timeless joy and beauty.

Although Libra is an air sign, there is a strong connection with the water element. Venus is exalted in Pisces, a water sign, which signifies unconditional love and compassion. The sea is a symbol of the subconscious workings of the mind, the psyche, and the deep emotional levels.

Foam, which is water intertwined with air, represents a soft approach, the blending of form and matter. As a Venusian you have the ability to adapt yourself to ever-changing conditions. Venus rules the curves that make the body sensual as well as the arches in architecture that create beauty and harmony. She depicts the power of response and receptivity. In astrology she rules what is most valued, how you give and receive love.

The attraction of the sexes is ruled by Venus. Venus is magnetic, and as Venusians you want to love and be loved. You are very alluring. It is the essential core of your being. Everything connected with love and commitment is of interest to you. You love old-fashioned courtship; the flowers, the candy, the movie or theater tickets—all of these small things mean a lot to you and if someone wants to impress you that person needs to know this about you. And let's not forget good food! Librans are connoisseurs and enjoy the best things in life.

Even though you are basically a sagacious thinker, when it comes to love you throw caution to the wind and jump in. You are very romantic and you get caught up in expectations. Slow down and give it the time it needs. Go with the flow, don't project what you want on a relationship until it's had time to unfold naturally.

Librans are irresistible to the opposite sex. You know how to charm and when you want to meet someone you are fearless in your approach. Your good mind always has a plan ready. But you must be careful, there is a tendency to let your imagination run unabated and picture only what you want to see. Cupid's arrows can really get the adrenaline going and good judgment falls by the wayside.

Naiveté in relationships creates disappointment. It's funny how fast you can jump into a relationship when you're so slow in making other commitments. Not that you're so easy to please. There is no one on earth who meets your ideals exactly, and rarely does anyone fulfill your expectations. Be sure you look before you leap. Romantic fantasy is a trap. As long as you see what you want to see, you'll be disappointed and pay a sad price for your imaginings. Without the ability to evaluate the situation realistically, you will always be looking for love, lamenting about a lost love, or in a problematic relationship. It is hard for you as a thinking type to trust your instincts, and yet for all that, in your heart of hearts you know that love is worth the risk.

There is a natural rhythm to relationships that takes you naturally to commitment, if there is enough compatibility there. Yet I have seen Librans get fainthearted and back off when everything is on target and there is no reason to. Why you vacillate is probably because you are always looking for *the perfect one,* and there is no such thing. Or this hesitation comes from knowing that you're not perfect either and your lover will surely reject you. You are good at sitting on your side of the fence waiting for your partner to make the first move. Fear of rejection and just plain not knowing how to move forward romantically can ruin a relationship. When emotions come into the picture, they tip your bucket. We humans are all emotional creatures and live our lives through our feelings. This fear of emotion has to be dealt with. Listen to your heart. Learn to express your true feelings—let others know you at your deepest level. You are good at writing. Write a poem or a note for your lover and let it tell your deepest wishes and fears. The words will come and it gets easier after a while to be there for yourself and own your feelings.

True love has movement—it must move forward or it stagnates. There is divine order in the universe, and when you are able to get into the flow of this perfect order, you attract everything you need. Trust your ability to make good decisions and all that comes with that.

A good marriage between two adults and the intimacy that ensues is a profound stirring of the soul. Yet it's sort of like opening Pandora's box. Often all the things you set great store in before marriage slowly disintegrate. You have no recourse but to honor the mysteries that are in each person's behavior. Libra is a very profound sign and it is your soul purpose to find the balancing point. Do not be swayed by sentiment. Remember Venus is from the sea, a symbol of emotion, and your intuitive body will support you unerringly if you don't try to interfere with or attempt to control it.

With all your consuming interest in love you may come to find out that relationships are basically problematic. A relationship that starts out so well, even after there is a certain amount of surety, can suddenly go south. You may never know why. Even the best of romances have their down time or just end suddenly. More than 75 percent of relationships never work out and 60 percent of marriages fail. I wonder sometimes if marriages are meant to last.

We learn more about ourselves in a relationship than we do in any other way. Maybe that is why we have so many of them. We learn more from the ones that don't work. But there is a time when you graduate from trying to make love happen and then your chances go up into the higher percentages of success. You have a fighting chance of creating something lasting when you are mature enough to be honest with yourself. Work on freeing yourself of ambivalence and fantasy. Remember there is no one more loving than you. A good self-image is essential to tolerate the anxieties that a courtship brings for everybody.

Sooner or later, good comes to those who do good; joy comes to those who bring humor to others; opportunity comes to those who persist in their dreams.

Your Nature Is Airy and Thoughtful

You are an air sign, which rules the thinking function. You want everything to add up mentally.

As a Libran, you not only have the male attribute of thinking but also the feminine attributes of grace and balance. These two components whirl in a constant dance, creating a highly intelligent objectivity. You naturally understand there are two sides to every situation and you also like to negotiate a resolution. You are very frustrated when your partner isn't as objective as you are. Even if your partner is an air sign, you like to duel mentally and you really like to win. Librans want to be right and the truth is you most often are. But you must lighten up or your lover will get turned off. Let someone else win every now and then.

The air signs like to relate life experiences to a preconceived framework of ideas. You have a highly developed mind, a sense of fairness, and an appreciation of structure and system. You adhere to principle and have a marked refinement in everyday life. You believe in justice and are exceedingly objective in everything you do. As a thinker you want all the facts. Oddly this is the sign that has a hard time making decisions. You like to be right but you don't want to enforce it. As a thinker emotions can overwhelm you. Feelings and emotions can't be classified, they aren't logical. This isn't to say that you aren't sensitive, you have very tender feelings. That's why it's easier to stay in your head. In this world of wounded relationships those who know how to relate emotionally are in the minority.

Relating on a Soul Level

The Chinese symbol of the yin, a feminine principle, and the yang, a masculine principle, is ruled by Libra.

You have seen the symbol many times: a black-and-white circular design that seems to whirl in a timeless dance. Yang, heaven, combines with yin, earth, to create all that comes to be.

Your soul is perfectly balanced and it is sacred. It's a personal sense of incompleteness that draws you to a relationship. We are always balancing the ego and the self. It is a constant process. The longing you have for a partner is really wanting to join with the other half of your own human wholeness. When you are balanced within yourself and the ego has made peace with the soul, you are able to be with someone else and experience joy.

Joy is an exultation of spirit and it is always there, waiting for your delight. On the other hand, happiness is fleeting; it is short-lived. If we are pursuing it, we never have it in our hands. As we live our lives we have happy moments, but to really enjoy our lives we must look deep within for a sacred space where we are balanced mentally and emotionally. If the purpose of life is to experience joy, then our goal must be to learn how to move into this peaceful dimension where joy resides.

Libra rules soulful acts of balance, yet it takes a leap of faith to bond with another person. You are looking for a sense of being mutually complete. You must have respect for the complexities of others and look for the soul of your commitment, where trust and commitment will weather all challenges and setbacks. When you can go to this space of true understanding, then love isn't such a risk, and you will be better off together than apart.

Although your air sign rules commitment, if the pressure is too extreme, you become emotionally pulled apart and bow out. It's hard for you to confront what you don't like, so you either evade or hold back emotionally. One of Libra's gifts is compromise, but it must be without losing decisiveness or personal integrity. When you're indecisive your life becomes so confused it becomes very difficult. Oddly, Libra always has to learn how to have personal relationships. You'll never be really happy on a soul level without a commitment. The answer is to move past the indecision—surrender the outcome and open your heart to the message of your soul. When this happens you magnetically attract just the right one.

Blocking Yourself from Love

Love is what a Libra thinks about, and in your secret heart of hearts, you long for the perfect romance.

Fanciful dreams are an important part of their psyche. When a person with qualities that you admire appears and you fall in love, you fall hard. Your opposite sign, Aries, is at play here giving you that spark of interest that gets you moving. As the sign of unity and balance you are naturally open to relationships. Without a partner you feel lost—there is something missing in being alone that you never really fulfill by yourself. Your cohort, Gemini, another air sign, has some of this also; they like to be coupled. Gemini is looking for fun events to share; however, you Librans are much more serious than that—you want soul connection. Libras don't fall in love too easily; you are very discriminating about who is right for you. When someone comes along who is on your vibration, you want to check it out. You instinctively know that two hearts are better than one.

Librans never date casually. Many times you are looking for the ring and planning the marriage after the first kiss. That is where the challenge of romantic fantasy begins. You have the right idea in some way; why waste your time on casual dating? You usually know what you need and want in a relationship from day one. You understand that intention is everything. You also know to only date people who are good marriage material, especially ones who are available, and you know that a good rule of thumb is that most people let you know very early in a relationship what their intentions are. The problem is that because you are such a linear thinker you move ahead of the phase you're in and go all the way to commitment after a few successful dates. This type of thinking brings several different scenarios that can ruin the relationship.

1. You go into fantasy and assume that your partner is feeling the same without real spoken verification.

2. You shut down out of fear of rejection and become emotionally frozen; you hide out in your head.

3. You vacillate, wanting to rush into commitment, then hold back until you're too confused to make a decision.

There are some Librans who can't make a commitment at all and need professional help. You need to let the relationship unfold on its own, through the normal relationship checkpoints, then the fear goes away.

These reactions can be changed when you learn to give up romantic notions in early courtship and let it unfold naturally. This is definitely possible with a Libra. You are a patient and considerate person first of all, but you must learn to be as considerate of yourself as you are of others.

Remember, until a relationship is bonded, dating is more about yourself than anything else. True love is created. There are magic moments in courtship, but true love evolves with time and trust, based on reality. If you want to hurry and shortcut this stage of discrimination, it comes back to haunt you. When you honestly face the humanness—the frailties—of your partner and love him anyway, you really fall in love. A real bond is forged.

It's important to say at this time that there are Librans who are such perfectionists that they give up on finding a relationship, yet seldom is a Libran really happy without a commitment of some sort. Your expectations are very high and not many people can fit your picture of what you expect from a mate.

When this occurs over and over it is plain to see that your perspective is off. Relationships are created, they don't come fully developed. This creates great unhappiness and needs to be addressed by seeking professional help. When your mind is so programmed by early childhood dysfunctions or you've suffered from a lot of unhappy relationships, it's hard to sort it out by yourself. Your nature is to be happy with a partner. Some of the healing can come from just following the phases of a courtship and understanding where you are. Of course good communication is always the answer.

As the lover of the zodiac, you must learn how to hold on to your own identity. Libra rules balance. You are always striving to see what is needed in order to maintain harmony and poise. In this process it's very important for you to realize that wholeness includes yourself. With your adaptable nature and your loving ways you can give too much and throw yourself off balance. The love of peace has a underlying meaning of winning a battle. The battle of integrating your mind with your feelings is a prerequisite to having a good relationship. After this hard-won battle you are equipped to join the battle of the sexes, which is alive and well on earth at this time. Libra wants to see the good and doesn't like to face the disharmony that the vulnerability of love enacts. Yet it is in this very act of love and the stress that it opens up, that our ego is refined with the soul.

A Libra Love Story

As a Libra you are so enamored with the idea of love and partnering that you project what you want to see onto your partner.

Dating can be a psychologically painful process. I heard of a Libran man who had been burned by love so many times that he had a *long* list of questions that his potential dates had to answer before he would go out with them. He didn't want to waste any more time—or money, too, we might guess. The amazing part is there were women who agreed to take the test. He married one of them.

In your compelling desire to be in a relationship, it's easy to jump to conclusions. Even though you are a perfectionist in most things, when you move into your feelings it's hard for you to set good boundaries. Libra is of the opinion that love is all. You need feedback from friends and family on their love lives. In your kind way you see the good and ignore the problems. I say ignore because you are so insightful and smart you really know the problem areas in an unconscious way. It's painful when you finally wake up and realize you knew it all the time, but didn't want to face it.

I know a Libran woman who met a lovely man at a party. She had been divorced for several years and was ready to start over with a new relationship. They did all the right things. They dated a long time before they were physically intimate. They slowly combined their friends and met each other's families. This is point where the relationship went wrong. They got carried away by romance and moved in together without making a real commitment and discussing long-range plans. They made a decision in Cancer's fourth phase of courtship, which is exclusivity and is still a courting stage.

It was too early for them to discuss their long-range plans because at that point they didn't know each other well enough.

Everything seemed wonderful on the outside. Their love was blossoming. Later, when the phases of evaluating and making a real commitment came up, their lives were so intertwined, literally, as far as work and money were concerned that they were afraid to speak out and let the other person know their doubts and concerns.

The truth is that while they had much in common and their life together was very compatible, they discounted the need for a true commitment. The relationship was pressured by lack of definition. She projected onto her partner her own feelings and took it for granted he was with her emotionally. She didn't get the feedback she needed from him. Actually he admired her so much that he put her on a pedestal, which separated them further. It may feel good to be worshipped, but that's not an equal and balanced union, which is what it takes to bond in the Aquarian age. Real love is nose to nose and toe to toe. Besides, you can be setting yourself up to be pushed off that pedestal when you least expect it.

The ending was dramatic and very unhappy for both of them.

In a serious relationship you're forced into looking at yourself. It is imperative that you see your partner realistically as well. You understand that everyone has a dark side, the side you don't like, and it's not likely to change. Relationships always mirror the things about ourselves that are suppressed in our subconscious. All relationships are karmic. To develop a good relationship you must resolve issues not only from this life but from past lives. Self-forgiveness is the only way to heal this karma. As you forgive yourself, your partner's frailties seem less challenging. Once you can see how you are alike and how you're different, then you can align with trust and love.

Your Most Authentic Self

As a Libran you understand balance.

It is your gift to be able to understand the subtleties of life. You are the artists of the zodiac—the art of the impressionists is a Libran's dream. By not acknowledging and using your power you waste a lot of time. Your gift of cooperation is not to give up your power. It's to be actively responding with all your power to make something work.

Just trying to be a good person must be replaced with making loving decisions even when there is stress involved. Confusion comes when you're learning a karmic lesson. By taking responsibility for your part of the karma, confusion fades and your good mind comes back with the answers you need. Your opposite sign, Aries, has the elements that you need to come into balance. Remember, by nature your male and female qualities are balanced. Libra is not a passive sign. Learning how to make strategies is an important part of your evolvement. You are a warrior of justice and yet you have a tender, compassionate heart. When you know that *you are love,* then you can make the concrete demands that you so rightly deserve.

October 23–November 22

Scorpio in Love

ELEMENT: Water
QUALITY: Fixed
PLANET: Mars and Pluto
STONE: Topaz
COLORS: Deep red and purple
ANIMALS: Scorpion, snake, eagle, and
               the phoenix
FLOWER: Anemone
LOVE WORDS: You're mine!

Gift — Responsiveness
Challenge — Emotional Avoidance

When a Scorpio Falls in Love

Scorpios are deeply passionate, and when you decide to share your life it is with an earnest connection, one that reaches the highest level of commitment and trust.

Scorpio, as the ruler of the eighth house, rules benefits from partnerships. But it is much more than that—it is a sign of transformation so deep that it goes all the way down into the cellular level. One of the benefits of the eighth house is sex, and Scorpios do have a reputation for passion. When you realize that it's not just sex you're interested in but something much deeper, you will get all you need in a relationship. You are passionate about everything you do, and with such intensity of feelings you have the endurance to make a partnership work on all levels. Being extremely affectionate and demonstrative, you are the happiest with a partner with whom you can combine emotional and sexual love.

You like to flirt with taboos. Scorpios love being powerful and are constantly looking for the upper hand. The more challenging the situation, the more you like it; your competitive nature thrives on rivalry. But it is critical to accept your partner without competition. True love demands a surrender on your part as well as theirs. Get your ego out of the way, and let your mind become attuned to a more sutble, spiritual view.

You are truly the happiest when you have a deep communion with nature and attune yourself to cosmic law. Your inquisitive nature desires to understand the mystery of life itself. You leave no stone unturned in your search for the underlying truth.

You must see love as a soulful experience. The true quest for you Scorpios is to bond with your own souls. However, this desire can be misconstrued and projected onto a person who has captured your imagination and represents your goal. It can become a burden for your loved one. Scorpio is a sign of extremes; you must learn to lighten up. In a positive sense the intensity of your sexual energy can be used as a means of uniting your ego with your soul, as well as uniting with the ego and soul of your loved one.

Only old souls come back as Scorpio. You have so much to learn, so much to process and release. Deep within you know this, but does it have to be so desperate and controlling?

There is a time in life that you come to terms with your passion and you're not so likely to look for this great love outside of yourself. When this happens you become patient and almost meek, a joy to be with and a loyal partner. Not to say, the younger and more passionate Scorpio isn't an exciting partner, but there is unrest and turbulence until you learn what you truly seek is within.

Love at first sight, which triggers such a deep response, doesn't always signal a lifelong relationship. Until you mature and are consciously ready to make a commitment you love the fascination and the challenge of love more than the end result. Your passionate and intense pursuit that so pleased your partner at the beginning may wane, and then with interest gone, you move out of the picture, leaving the person confused and rejected. You want to be transformed through love. You are responsive to the pull of sexual energy and can get caught up in the physical aspects of making love when deep inside you actually are seeking a more profound experience. A lot of sex addicts are Scorpios, looking for love in all the wrong places.

Scorpio is the sign of release, integration, and regeneration, and your nature is to control your environment to insure your desires will be met. Whereas a Libra is basically indecisive, always trying to do the right thing, an unevolved Scorpio is compulsively decisive and doesn't care at all what's right form.

Scorpio intensity sends out a powerful aura. When you enter a room your tremendous vitality is catching. You make powerful leaders and attract a support system. With such a deep need to transform everything within your reach, you must learn to be responsible for your impacting nature. You don't take things lightly and often find yourself reacting to your environment and the people around you with doubt and skepticism. Your ability to critique is a good trait that can turn against you. Snap judgments are dangerous for Scorpios.

When you finally understand the real intimacy of a true commitment, it is consummated with the highest level of emotional feeling possible and a need to bond that is so intense that your affections are not for the fainthearted.

You are capable of extreme self-sacrifice for those you

love. If any loved one is threatened in any way you feel it is your duty to attack, either verbally or physically—like a she-animal protecting her young. By being so insightful, you have good ammunition to attack, yet you must be very careful or your actions can be too harsh and you can hurt your loved ones instead of making them feel safe.

You are a terrible foe. You are powerful in how you project yourself and it's important to remember that you are responsible for your influence on others. You are a master of the silent treatment. If you really want to torture someone after a disagreement, you can be totally still and let that person stew in the confusion. Scorpio has great patience. Remember, the coiled snake is a symbol for Scorpio. You can wait a long time to get even.

Your symbol, the snake, is one of the oldest symbols for power in recorded history. It is very controversial—just like Scorpio. In many parts of the world it means great wisdom. In ancient times great kings sought out the Oracle of Delphi, who received her psychic answers from a great python. The Buddha sitting under a bodhi tree had a serpent coil around him seven times. The snake's encounter with the Buddha symbolized the cleansing of all his past life karma and, consequently, his enlightenment.

In the western world the snake is seen as evil. The belief is that it rules a dark part of our nature, which is called "the shadow." Since the subconscious where the shadow part of us resides is ruled by Scorpio, you mustn't allow your weaknesses to overpower your true wisdom.

In the story *The Little Prince,* as the prince gazes at the snake, he says at last, "You are a funny animal, you are no thicker than a finger."

"But I'm more powerful than the finger of a king," replies the snake.

There is no doubt, Scorpio, the use of power is your life issue.

When Scorpios operate out of a higher consciousness and

use the power of creation that is their natural birthright, they are the highest and most effective of all the signs.

You have a penchant for zeroing in on your partner's vulnerability. Control methods like this damage your relationship at a deep level. The tendency to be stubborn and controlling is what gives Scorpios their bad reputation. Your stubborn, vindictive ways must be rechanneled into understanding and forgiveness or you'll end up hurting a lot of people and creating some real bad karma for yourself. Remember, what goes around comes around!

Mars, which is Scorpio's first ruler, is aggressive, and with its influence comes strong physical desire. Pluto, the second ruler of Scorpio, rules the passion for life that gives us our survival instinct. You generally know what you want, and although you may not say a thing about it, your whole makeup is to move slowly in that direction and take action at just the right time. With maturity you learn how to pace your aggression so that the rewards mean more to you and there is a likelihood of creating the lasting relationship you so deeply desire.

One of the main things you need to merge comfortably into a relationship is the space to learn. There is an unwritten law in the universe that says don't press a Scorpio. It's like taking a tiger home to dinner. Having space isn't opposite from being intimate. You must have room to allow intimacy to happen. A sexual attraction stays fresh and new when you come together as two distinct, separate poles. You must see the conflicts as part of the dance. Your partner always reflects you in some way and your conflicts help you identify and contact essential missing parts of yourself. With more awareness and the space needed, you allow love to flow through you in a free and unobstructed way.

With all this intensity, when you fall in love you want it to last. You hold back emotionally at first, knowing that if you do allow someone to enter into your heart that person is there for a long time. Scorpios hold on to relationships and their desire is to make them work. Even after the love and attraction is long gone, you are prone to stay in a relationship, daring to hope you still might work it out.

Your Nature Is Watery and Intuitive

Water exists in three states: in its natural state it is fluid—this is Cancer, a sign of creation; when frozen it becomes solid— this rules strong-willed Scorpio; when heated it is vaporous— this is metaphysical Pisces.

As a three-dimensional water sign, you are in touch with the subtleties that others don't even notice. You are an insightful person and it helps to support your relationships.

Your emotions range from deep passion and overwhelming fears to feeling euphorically at one with creation. Quite a range of feelings, but you more often than not keep your own counsel. Scorpio knows instinctively that sexual energy can be channeled in many directions, sex is only one. Scorpio is really a sign of controlled response. Look at a snake coiled in attack. It can hold its position for a long time. It takes a lot of will to stop nature's tide; that is why you Scorpios are so powerful. You have the ability to pull honesty down to the tightest point there is.

As the most stationary condition of all the water signs you seem very calm on the outside. This is very deceptive. Your vulnerability to hurt is so pronounced that you may be imploding on the inside and easily thrown off course. By realizing the true nature of your emotional longing, which is your need for love, and making yourself available to your loved ones, you are assured of increasing inner contentment as the years pass. Your desire to bond with your loved one is a primary need, even though it is a slow and often a painful process. Even as a Scorpio with all your intensity and persuasiveness there are no guarantees.

There is a wonderful day when a Scorpio knows deep within his or her soul that all the focus on outer pursuits is in vain.

> Serene I fold my hands and wait,
> Nor care for wind or tide nor sea:
> I rave no more 'gainst time and fate,
> For lo! my own shall come to me.
> —John Burroughs, *Waiting*

Relating on a Soul Level

Scorpio is intently complex and soulfully enigmatic.

As the strongest sign of emotional power in the zodiac you are bound by your very nature to undergo intense emotional experiences, like the ocean in a storm. Even if you are a great actor—and, by the way, many Scorpios are—you can't hide the power that emanates from your very soul, and yet many of you never accept the power that is rightly yours. No other sign of the zodiac is so deeply insightful and capable of such far-reaching effects on environment. You hang between multiple worlds and, like a great shaman that journeys to the edge and expands the possibilities, you can reconnect the life force with everything you do.

Magical forces and vast regenerative powers are at play here, like the alchemist patiently mixing potions to change base metal into gold. There is a deep desire in a Scorpio's soul to transform and to be transformed.

To make your intense nature even more complex, there is a battle being fought between your lower senses and your soul. You have a deep-seated desire to go to the depth, to be renewed and rise to the heights. As your desires are purified and you understand transcendence, you can accomplish great things. Your gift is great emotional power. This power can either be used constructively to achieve regeneration or be your own worst enemy, destroying the things you want the most. With your desire to conquer the material world, eliminating everything that is not conducive to higher purpose, or be conquered by it, you can eliminate yourself from your field of dreams. But Scorpio is a transcendent sign; he rules things that can't be seen. Your subconscious is the most powerful thing you have. That open contact with the inner working of the subconscious is where most of your power lies.

Blocking Yourself from Love

With a Scorpio, desire (fire) and emotion (water) rule supreme.

Sir Roger L'Estrange in Aesop 38 said: "It is with our passions, as it is with fire and water, they are good servants but bad masters." Scorpio rules the passions of sex, power, and money. In defense of Scorpio, anything worth doing has passion connected to it. Trusting your hunches is more effective than trying to control events with your intellect or will. Passion is life's drama, it has to do with emotion, and how it unfolds is usually not reasonable. I have always seen passion as emotion's highest inspiration. Unless you have a deep consuming interest that tests your skill and patience you're not a full-fledged Scorpio. Scorpios are great golfers for this reason and they are passionate about it. It's not just a game to them.

Either way, whether passion is positive and creates something healing, or negative and does more harm than good, it has to do with the vulnerability of your emotions. You must surrender to the psychic forces that move to bring about cleansing experiences, revelations, and corrections. No matter how you buttress yourself against the world and temper your response, your opponent is very near; it's probably yourself. Wasn't it Pogo, the comic strip character and probably a Scorpio, who said, "I have met the enemy and he is us"?

Sex, power, and money are the consistent themes of Scorpio. You are easily aroused and aggressive in sexual matters. Money is a big turn-on for you. Just like your co-heart, Aries, also ruled by Mars, when you're interested in any subject, person, place, or thing, you're intensely interested—there is no moderation in your sign. What you really need here is discretion and restraint. Since your sign rules benefits from partners, you sooner or later have to face the fact that being destructive when cornered is not your best decision. Don't bite the hand that feeds you. You are complex, Scorpio! And you have many conflicting thought processes to sort out.

- You want to be a loner, yet your desire to be seen and heard circumvents this desire.

- Your desire to be right and win at every turn gives other people power over you.

- You can never totally escape from others' opinions, even though you have amazing diversionary tactics.

- As the devil's advocate you love to disappoint expectations.

- You're much softer than you act and lead people astray on purpose.

This is where Scorpios fake themselves out the most. They seek out a private place and isolate themselves mentally, emotionally, and physically. Many times this is with the highest intentions. You want to protect your environment and your loved ones or simply have rest time, but how can your loved ones know you if you are removed from them, no matter what your intentions are? You learn through experiences how to relate to others. By learning cooperation out of respect for the rights of your partner, you develop the self-control of trust and real intimacy.

In a materialistic way Scorpio is very powerful. Other people's money comes to you. Many of you inherit money and you're good at saving money, particularly as an investor. You like to feel safe, much like your opposite sign, Taurus, and you focus on creating a sound financial base. Many top CEOs are Scorpios, particularly in areas of finance. Your motivation for financial success gives you the grounded position you need egowise. From a secure financial position it is possible for you develop the self-esteem that leads to surrender of the ego. After this ascent into power you often learn what power really is, and your final reward for such perseverance is being able to go to great spiritual heights.

You are never parsimonious, but you can't bear incompetence or sloth and will fearlessly and sometimes ruthlessly clean up the problems you see around you. Many surgeons are Scorpios; it suits your sign's courageous nature to cut open the body so it can be healed. Pluto in mythology was the brother of Neptune. He ruled the masses and was man's judge who punished when necessary. As a Scorpio you inherently believe in justice. Good should be rewarded and evil punished. Bobby Kennedy was a Scorpio and he attacked the Mafia, a dark Scorpio symbol, as is the Internal Revenue Service, by the way. Perhaps he was naive in his thinking that he could challenge the darkest system around and not be harmed.

When you have made your success you know how to share with others. It has to come on your own terms and there usually is a lesson with it. Look at Scorpio Bill Gates—it took him a while to part with some of his money. The motivational focus needs to be changed from aggression and survival to safety and abundance.

Being successful professionally usually works out very well for you; you always love a challenge and will take it to the end. It's the vulnerable part of your nature that is fearful. Your way of reacting to fear is to freeze. You might see yourself as invisible, but Scorpios stand out in a crowd, no shrinking violets here. Besides, you have such beautiful eyes that you draw people in. To release fear you must open your heart. This isn't so easy when your mind is racing and you're in a reactive position.

Your nature is cautious, you move slowly, until the moment of attack, then with great precision you hit your mark. Your contentious nature must be tempered. You need to back off and calm down, often your fears are not founded. When you feel the need to control others and allow emotional pressure to build up, rather than controlling your own sensual and emotional excesses, you can explode into total lack of self-control. Or implode and fall into deep despair or depression. An openhearted talk with your loved one does wonders.

Libra, the sign of commitment, has inner conflicts that are mental, whereas Scorpio's conflict is deeply emotional. With so much emotional turbulence it's not easy to be a Scorpio. The early astrology books say that only old souls come back into the earth plane as Scorpios. By digging down through the dregs of past-life karma and the pain of early childhood, you have a chance to move forward on your soul path. There is a time, after years of conflict, when you move past the severe challenges that life presents; you enter a place of great honesty. Then strength and healing power become your very essence.

Loyalty is one of your best traits and you have almost superhuman ways of facing facts. Even if the investigation is unpleasant you never recoil. Your probe is solid, thorough, and deep. Yet your methods border on being downright destructive. I always say that Scorpio is to the point. Scorpios have weapons, supplied by your animal rulers: the scorpion's stinger, the snake's fangs, and the eagle's talons. Watch out or you will jab the ones you love the most, and for what purpose other than to satisfy this relentless part of your nature?

There is a wonderful (Scorpio) story about a scorpion who asked a turtle for a ride to the other side of the lake. The scorpion begged and pleaded, promising over and over that he wouldn't sting him. Finally the turtle loaded him up and swam off with the scorpion on his back. When they were halfway across, of course, the scorpion fatally stung the turtle. As they were sinking to their watery grave he asked the scorpion why he did it knowing full well that he would die as well. The scorpion replied, "It's my nature."

Your nature must be tempered or you too will end up at the bottom of the lake or alone on the mountain like the eagle, with such high altitude that there is no oxygen, and no one to love either for that matter.

A Scorpio Moment

I am a Scorpio observer.

I have said if there is a Scorpio around I can hear his tail rattling. I never take the warning; as a Capricorn I find Scorpios the most fascinating of all the signs. I have some scars, that's true, but I've also been deepened emotionally by these wonderfully creative and fearless people. I feel that with my Capricorn nature I wouldn't have scratched the surface on intimacy without my Scorpio friends. It helps that in my natal chart I have Jupiter, the planet of good luck, in Scorpio.

Scorpio rules much more than just your emotional responses. Scorpio rules things that can't be seen but that you know are there already. Pluto, the second planetary ruler of Scorpio, represents the underworld of man's unconscious, those elements in his nature that have not yet been redeemed and integrated with the rest of his being. Pluto's job is to bring to the surface hidden conditions that have lain dormant in the subconscious so that they can be transformed into a new source of power. Pluto was found in 1930, at the same time atomic energy was discovered. That gives you an idea of power.

In Greek mythology, Pluto was the god of the underworld.

Can't you just see this darkly handsome warrior with a red cape, coming out of a fissure in the earth, in a chariot with a glittering team of horses, intently focused on taking his true love home with him. He was lonely with all his riches and needed someone to nourish and adore him. The story goes that in a ruthless Scorpio fashion Pluto abducted the young and innocent Persephone, a Taurian earth goddess, and took her to his castle deep down inside the earth. Persephone liked him well enough, it seems, to eat six pomegranate seeds, although she had been warned not to eat anything. However, after her mother, Demeter (the goddess of nature), furiously intervened, Persephone was permitted to come back up in the spring. Because of her indiscretion she was forced to spend the winters with Pluto underground. Pretty exciting! Women often like those deep, dark, mysterious types. This myth is the archetype for many love fantasies. Their combined energies were very compatible, the story of nature itself. The fruitfulness of nature (Taurus) and the underground root systems (Scorpio) are needed for the growth of crops. The story has a message that surprise, passion, and hidden moments are just as important a part of the courtship process as practical assessment. Pluto was the god of great riches. Think of all the priceless wealth under the ground—oil, gas, uranium, and myriad other treasures that the earth holds in her bosom. Persephone was happy with Pluto and never complained about her abduction. The dark can be intertwined with the light.

Famous beauty and award-winning actress Julia Roberts is a Scorpio. Have you ever noticed that movie stars often gets typecast in roles that are really significant for their own growth? You can almost guess their Sun signs by the roles they play. One of Julia's most famous roles was the young, misplaced call girl in the movie *Pretty Woman*. The Plutonian character played by Richard Gere, a wealthy man who was ruthlessly involved in buying up small companies and disseminating them for money, lured her into the underground of the Beverly Hills Hotel and Rodeo Drive. Sex, power, and money all right. What's a nice girl like Julia doing in a place like that? Shopping, of course! And with her Persephone goddess ways she lured him into her life, sans her call girl status, of course, and he was transformed by her basically good ethics. Unbelievable, maybe, but the myth is there. I wonder how long that relationship lasted. But the story was so much fun, the sex so sweet, and the jokes were so clever. A real Scorpio moment.

Your Most Authentic Self

You're a very old soul, Scorpio.

It's not easy to be pulled in so many directions, called forth from past lives to the present. The present is hard enough as it is. You are lucky to have forceful Mars and transforming Pluto as your rulers. Especially if you understand that Mars represents the principle that compels a person to take positive action—the warrior's approach of transcendence.

When you are focused and balanced no matter how deep the karmic wounds, you are capable more than any other sign of achieving a major breakthrough in this lifetime.

- Your spiritual path is to go from darkness into light, and your destiny is to destroy the ego's hold on your mind.

- You will become conscious of the redundancy of returning to earth with the same old lesson once again.

- You learn how to transform karma's desperate hold by claiming your soul's wisdom and grace.

- You must look out for choices that will bring regret.

- You are one of the seekers of the zodiac and you will never be truly at peace with yourself until you find your own path of light.

To open the heart is a spiritual practice that must be imbibed daily. There are many routes to this level of consciousness and you must seek your own. A Scorpio keeps his or her own counsel, and perhaps that is the best way. There is no easy or logical way to purge your very soul; you have to come to it in your own good time. Yet it is possible to master your shadow side. It never goes away completely, but after you move from a sense of fear to knowing you are safe and in God's hands, you won't lose your equilibrium. After this ego transcendence you develop the insight that heals the people around you. Your partner has grown accustomed to your mysterious ways and is nourished by your deep attention and concern. In the myth of Pluto, after people had been tested and judged to see if the good outweighed the evil, they were taken to a place of happiness called the Elysian Fields. Perhaps Persephone was able to create beauty down inside the earth. You don't have to actually die to be reborn. You can have beauty, peace, and abundance daily as you learn to be transformed here on earth.

November 23–December 21

Sagittarius in Love

ELEMENT:	Fire
QUALITY:	Mutable
RULER:	Jupiter
STONE:	Turquoise
COLOR:	Orange
ANIMALS:	Large animals
FLOWER:	Dahlia
LOVE WORDS:	Blow in my ear and I'll follow you anywhere!

Gift — Enthusiasm
Challenge — Independence

When a Sagittarius Fall in Love

When Sagittarius falls in love it's a blastoff in search of a new world.

You are a fire sign, remember, and fire has many aspects. From ember to flame you have to learn how to manage the intensities of your desires. A Sag is independent and has been called the bachelor sign of the zodiac. Unless it's worth your while you're not interested in partnering. You are perfectly happy pursuing your own interests. Being such a healthy specimen of nature you are physically attuned to sex and you're not immune to love's call. Happily you understand that to really love someone you have to like them too, or your relationships could be superficial and self-gratifying.

Many Sagittarians fall in love with friends. You make friends easily and one of your best traits is that you're not judgmental. You're often so busy with your life that the perfect mate could be sitting right next to you and you haven't noticed. But when you're ready you are fearless in your pursuit, and your enthusiasm can fuse two into one. You take risks in love and even though the pleaser side of you is afraid of rejection, you push on, knowing deep inside that where there's fear there's also power and this power leads to creating something wonderful.

Sagittarius is a sign of communication, and relationships are everything to you. You operate at a level where all interaction is simple, direct, and rich with an immediacy of response to human feeling and individual needs. You have a creative approach to love, a keen sense of attention to details, an objective technique of give and take, and you want to love and be loved back. Yet you must have feedback. A Sag is lost without a response. When you are an emotionally and spiritually advanced Sag, the healing balm of love is of constant interest and total immersion into a commitment is your forte. You have the ability to revel in this kind of relationship and find each day as stimulating as the first. Your love is always new to you, always vibrant with fresh vitality, and unique even in the challenge of everyday living. Sagittarians are notoriously gun-shy when it comes to commitment, basing so much value on personal freedom, you might think they would be immune to romance. Not true! Sagittarians marry just like everyone else and sometimes more than once. I tell them they will keep doing it until they get it right. With your reactive nature it's important for you to slow things down and be sure. You won't stay in a relationship that's wrong. Warning! Sometimes you don't do what is needed to heal a relationship. The outcome of leaving too fast is that the same problem shows up in the next person and there you go again.

Each stage of courtship is important and you don't have to lose interest when things slow down. Short attention spans are signs of immaturity. The antidote for Sag is to stay present in the real world; there is always a need for you to get grounded in the facts. It's easy for you to be grounded in the near conscious—a state of mind that's between the conscious mind and the unconscious. When you've come to terms with what's really going on underneath and what you need to do to solve the problem, you are as loyal as a puppy. And once the courtship is said and done and the commitment is made, you Sagittarians come home to roost like the other signs— you just like to know that the gate is open.

Your Nature Is Fiery and Expressive

Fire is the vital spirit that keeps us in motion; it inspires us and reunites us with the source of all being.

The element of fire is necessary in the process of transformation. The ancient alchemists used it to fuse the other elements of water, earth, and air in hopes of transforming the ego into the self. Fire rules the feelings of how we relate to what is happening around us, and on a higher plane it rules the divinity within us.

As a fire sign you are excitable with an eye out for safety. There is a nervous verve to your nature, an excitability that makes your color high and your reactions quick. You retain the sensitivity of spirit to know what is going on around you at all times. Like the horse, you have a wide span of peripheral vision. In times long ago when horses ran free they were fearless; now domesticated horses are completely reliant on their masters. What a well-trained horse has lost in fearless independence is made up for in the power and loyalty she gives to her owner.

As a fire sign, Sagittarians are very expressive, words flow from their lips and they have a great ability to tell a stirring story and entertain their friends; many famous writers have Sagittarius prominent in their charts. You have a great need to spread the truth. Your thinking is inspired and your charisma is infectious.

Just watch out when you are tired; the fire signs can be rascals when stirred up and they usually have a temper. Yet, of all the fire signs, Sagittarians are the most reasonable, being so conscious of others' needs while in tune with their surroundings.

All the fire signs are prone to egocentric behavior. Fire signs are always me first. But as a Sag, you are also seeking. Your inner desire is to know about your soul. First comes the quest for self-knowledge, then travel to foreign lands and the study of new ideologies, finally comes the phase of finding a teacher you can identity with or a philosophy to devote yourself to. After all the wondering you can sit at home with your heart full of love and wisdom and share your wondrous knowledge with your wife, children, grandchildren, and many friends. Sagittarians are too energetic to be lazy and often start enterprises late in life to keep active.

Relating on a Soul Level

The seal of Sagittarius is the rainbow.

The rainbow contains all the basic colors, from red to purple, and indicates a balancing of the seven chakras. The chakra points reside in the body from the base of the spine to the top of the head. They are constantly in motion and vibrate with creative energy. Sagittarius is aware of the process of moving from the animal nature, the lower chakras, to the spiritual nature, the higher chakras. The Hindus say when all of the chakras are opened and cleared the person moves into higher levels of consciousness. The rainbow has all the colors of the chakras lined up in perfect order and is a message of spiritual attainment.

"The rainbow is more beautiful than the end of it, because the rainbow is now. And the pot never turns out to be quite what you expected."
—Author unknown

The gold at the end of the rainbow is God and symbolizes your peace of mind. If you seek anything else you will be disappointed. With this auspicious and beautiful symbol, you are born with a highly conscious mind that likes to join with others in worship. You seek the highest knowledge. But when your chakras are shut down through fear and disappointment, your energy level is low and there is little joy in your life experience. Your sign rules the changeover from nature to higher consciousness. You are blessed with the ability to see subtleties and give great insights. Sagittarius is a sign of psychological and spiritual growth, and it pulls no punches. When your opinion is needed, the undiluted truth, in your eyes, literally jumps out of your mouth.

The ancient pictorial representation for Sagittarius is the centaur who lifts a bow toward the heavens and is about to speed an arrow straight to its mark. Perhaps the gaze of the centaur and the arrow point to Jupiter, Sagittarius's ruler, who resides at the top of Mount Olympus. Half horse, half man, Sagittarius has the lithe, active body of the horse and the directed attitude of the man. The horse connects you with the earth and the world of instinct and the man with his heavenly intent suggests distant worlds and galaxies. This combination of horse and man in search of enlightenment brings an earthy good nature and a happy-go-lucky temperament.

Sagittarius is largely an animal-like spirit. Your sign rules the entrance into the animal kingdom and combines the intelligence of the human brain and the expressive animal-like joy of nature. Large animals are under Sagittarius's rule—

dogs and horses, also wild animals such as elephants, camels, giraffes, hippopotami, whales, and dolphins. Sagittarians have an open look much like a horse or deer, or a long-nosed dog. Your look is alert and has an ingenious frankness that attracts others and gives them a sense of well-being.

When I was in Thailand, my friends and I took an hour-long elephant ride through the jungle. I was amazed at how responsive the elephants were to our needs. When one of my friends dropped her purse, her elephant gracefully picked it up with his trunk and gently put it back in her lap. We were all delighted by this gentlemanly effort.

As I was enjoying the ride I felt a subtle movement of something encircling my body, a palpable feeling of warmth slowly surrounded me. The elephant was sending me a big hug, responding to my elation. I must say that was a marvelous experience. I have Sagittarius rising in my chart, so it's not so unusual for me to love animals, but I was overjoyed to get such an amazing response.

Love is a natural state for Sagittarians. You naturally know how to enjoy life. I sometimes call you collie puppies with floppy ears—spontaneous and alert to the needs of others yet soul bent on enjoying yourself no matter what is really happening around you.

You Sagittarians have a positive attitude no matter what, so you're not usually around when others need emotional support. You're off to do something energetic and fun when the going gets rough. It's really one of your best characteristics, however, that you don't enable a situation when you're not equipped to help. You're always there to love and support when your partner has cleared out his feelings, it's just that you won't let anyone pull you down. There is such an attitude of faith in God and nature that your philosophy is to be completely in the moment, just like an animal, and do what is at hand. No crying over the past for you! It's over, done, let's look ahead to the future. How about a walk on the beach?

Jupiter, the ruler of Sagittarius, is the sign of the great teacher and in India is called the Guru. Jupiter shows us what we trust, value, and desire as our highest goal It is the sign of the highest good. Again there are the two sides—one for the earthly desires of abundance, which we have every right to, and one for the gift of spiritual worthiness that comes from our connection to God.

Animals are full of grace and innocence. All animals experience the need to survive, and yet their natural curiosity urges them on and they maintain a joyous presence. My little dog Tasha is always happy to see me even if I've only been gone for a few minutes. When I'm lucky enough to be with the dolphins that swim off my beach, they come up to the boat with smiling faces and look me in the eye, as if to say, "I'm so glad you're here." Sagittarius rules this joyous state of happiness. When you maintain your soul connection, your natural gift is a deep connection to nature and animals. It's a joy to spend time with you. You brighten any situation you are in. When you are in a relationship with the right partner this ecstasy is ever present and the downright fun you have together brings you closer each day. When you take the risk of intimacy you enhance this state, although it is harder for you than other signs. You like to *be* happy, not to talk about it.

Blocking Yourself from Love

A Sagittarius person must have a guiding philosophy of life to have a core sense of meaning and purpose.

There is a deep-seated desire within you to reach out to God's will. Your natural curiosity takes you on a soul search for most of your life. Your eyes are always on the future. You wonder what is going on somewhere else and chase after rainbows, forgetting they are within, in your seven chakras. Your dreams can take you over and keep you from living your life as it simply unfolds. You are fundamentally very restless. This is isolating; by always looking outside of yourself, you miss what is going on in the present moment. The positive events around you are overlooked. You always have an eye on the door.

The pursuit of happiness is one of your greatest gifts from God, but happy moments are brief and fleeting. Real joy has to be received from your deepest sense of inner meaning and purpose, in the activity of the moment of truth, you're living right now. We can have joy all the time if we change our perspective and, I might add, our values. The lesson you must learn is that joy is within, not in some distant country or philosophy. Your soul gives you messages in your daily surroundings, and if you're not careful your soul mate may show up while you're lost in your dreams.

With the two distinct sides of Sagittarius volleying back and forth between nature's call and higher principles, too much of your life is spent in vacillation. There is a tendency to put on an act. Ask Sagittarians how they are, and they'll all answer "Great," even if they're in the worst circumstances of their life. When you're separated from your soul, it's easy to fall into despair. When a Sag gets down it's a terrible thing. You seek isolation, you're like the lone roan on the hill watching over your herd. Like Scorpio and Capricorn there is a tendency to separate from others emotionally. All the signs of commitment from Libra to Pisces are prone to be objective. The innate need you have to share with others helps to keep you balanced. To truly honor the core of your existence is to be with your partner, sharing plans, ideals, and values. Sagittarius loves a joining of minds. Like Gemini, your opposite sign, you are looking for your lost twin, and when you find your love you vacillate between wanting total bonding and being afraid of loosing your freedom.

As a fire sign, when you are in courtship with someone you really like you want to go too fast. Like fire racing across a field you burn up all the fuel in one night. It's like gorging yourself on a beautiful meal and being so full you feel like re-gurgitating. You must learn to set reasonable boundaries, and the most important thing of all to learn is patience. Immerse yourself in the knowledge that you of yourself do nothing, that without a solid connection to your soul you are cut off from joy. One way to sustain a sense of peace is to be grateful at all times for your opportunity to experience life in every way.

A Sagittarius Love Story

I have found that Sagittarian relationships are hard to sustain because they start off so dramatically.

There is no way to keep up that sort of intensity. Like fire-works on the fourth of July, your relationships burst into light then drift down into little ashes. Sagittarian couples can enjoy long, compatible relationships if they learn to cut down on the artificial behavior that just feeds the ego. To have an enduring relationship you must go slowly, by wanting too much too quickly you may end up with nothing but broken dreams.

Sagittarians like to shock others. It is one of the signs of drama. Look at the animal kingdom and its surprising shapes and colors. A circus with the clowns and trained wild animals is ruled by Sag. Great spiritual leaders wear fantastic robes, and fashion magazines generally show you the most bizarre and unwearable clothes. This is all Sagittarian. If you watch a Sagittarius, sooner or later she will show up in something that gets your attention. Look at Sagittarian Bette Midler with her flair for zany and flamboyant costumes. If you fall in love with a Sag be prepared to be shocked by your partner's spontaneity and don't be surprised if he goes off and does his thing without you every now and then. Sagitarians never want to give up their sense of adventure and independence.

John F. Kennedy Jr. was a perfect Sagittarius. He loved

travel, sports, and the great outdoors. He had only been married a short time before he ran off on a solo trip to Iceland. He loved dramatic women and found Daryl Hannah (another Sag) a good companion for years. If his life had not ended so abruptly who knows what new ambitions were ahead for him, maybe even politics. Being born into wealth suits Sagittarians, and they know how to enjoy it. A Sagittarius can be ambitious for success, but it has to be fun too. Sagittarius in its highest state is very noble. Kennedy's marriage to Capricorn Carolyn Bessette was an amazing romance in that they were so different, but she did have a Sagittarius rising.

Another quintessential Sagittarius was the late Frank Sinatra. His love for Capricorn Ava Gardner gave him a muse to follow and kept his search for meaning alive all his life. His daring, sometimes outrageous lifestyle was front-page news. Although Sinatra and Kennedy were from different backgrounds, their love lives had parallels: first love, the girl next door; then a tempestuous love affair with a rare and beautiful star; then finally a sound social decision for a lifetime partner who has staying power—not quiet so dramatic but still very outstanding. With a Sag, people always wonder if it will last. The surprise is that Sagittarians will finally bond after they've had their fling—that is if they choose a mate that gives them free range.

Your Most Authentic Self

Sagittarius is a sign of prosperity; it rules the law of abundance and faith.

If you Sagittarians had a creed, it would be: Follow your instinct, find the answer day by day, moment by moment. As a master of creative concepts, you're never at a loss for an ideas and have tremendous stamina to carry out your goals.

You have an inner vibrancy that is light, free, and enthusiastic. You focus on the solution not the problem itself.

There is a tendency to exaggerate. This can be the punch line in a joke or an outright lie; this behavior is compensatory for feelings of inadequacy that are pushed down into the deep subconscious. Yet your good attitude wins. You are healed of your fears by consistently making positive choices and getting loving support from your companions.

When entering into a relationship, the very beginning is the best part for you. It's a peak experience. But it's hard to keep anything at such an intense level. Like Aries, your fire sign partner, your interest wanes. It is your lesson in life to slow down and listen to your feelings and ask about the feelings of your significant other. You don't have to spill your guts to be intimate. To be grateful for your partner's time and energy helps to make courtship an exciting experience. You need a partner who is mentally and philosophically stimulating. You are always learning something new and it's necessary for your partner to be interested in personal growth. When you have a feeling of inadequacy, if your partner listens to you and you listen to him there is a feeling of equity established, and you learn something.

In an interview, Sagittarian Steven Spielberg said that listening was the most important trait you can have. He added: "But it's the inner voice you listen for, not the voices on the outside." When asked what he would say to God when he went to heaven, if there is such a place, he replied, "Thanks for listening."

December 22–January 19

Capricorn in Love

ELEMENT:	Earth
QUALITY:	Cardinal
PLANET:	Saturn
STONE:	Garnet
COLOR:	Brown
ANIMAL:	Goat
FLOWER:	Holly
LOVE WORDS:	I'd climb the highest mountain!

Gift — Loyalty
Challenge — Isolation

When a Capricorn Falls in Love

Capricorn is analytical, somewhat detached, and rules the mature and responsible side to life. Yet you still get a bad rap in the love department.

So unfair! No one is more loyal and willing to work together to build a good relationship than Capricorn. When you fall in love it's for the long term. You take your time getting into a relationship because once you're in, you don't know how to get out. Moving up is your direction, not out. You are very conservative emotionally and it takes a while for you to open up, but if your partner gives you the time you need to feel, evaluate, and process, you can be the most grounded and sincere lover in the whole zodiac.

Capricorns are hard to read. You have an aloof manner that you assume to protect your sensitivity. This is a fragile front, as most Capricorns are actually very down-home once you get to know them. A Capricorn is motivated to achieve. Symbols change with the times and Capricorns seem to have sold their souls to the company store in this time of big business. You have lost the status of the god of harvest as it was in ancient times. The winter solstice, which begins in the Capricorn time of year, was the time of the Roman holiday called the Saturnalia, a holiday at the end of the year with great celebrations and fertility rites. The wine flowed like water. Many Capricorns still have a marvelous green thumb and grow their own tomatoes. There is a hint of the cornucopia of fruits and vegetables overflowing along with the gold.

The Greek word *Capricornus* means "goat horn." Capricorn is associated with the bones and especially with the knees. The Greek mythological association for Capricorn is the nymph Amalthea, whose goat suckled the newborn Jupiter, although some books say that Amalthea was the goat itself. The story goes that Jupiter broke off the horn of the goat and gave it to Amalthea and promised her she would be able to obtain anything she wished from the horn, or cornucopia. He set her image among the stars—the constellation Capricorn. This myth has a lot in it. Also, who would ever guess that the cornucopia was Capricorn? It sounds more like a Sagittarius symbol of abundance. Maybe Jupiter (a Sagittarian god) wanted an earth sign to guard the riches of the earth, and Saturn, the sea goat at the top of the mountain with all the experience, being Capricorn's ruler, is the perfect guardian of wealth. But it is wealth gained through hard work and wisdom rather than the instant remuneration of the horn of plenty as you might think.

There is a connection between the symbols for Sagittarius and Capricorn. If you turn Saturn (which looks like a 5) upside down, it becomes Jupiter (which looks like a 4); and if you turn Jupiter upside down, it looks like Saturn. Underneath Saturn's strict demeanor is the cornucopia, and by turning Jupiter over you have Saturn, which restricts after too much indolence. In other words, your luck can run out on you if you don't have the right values and discipline. And Saturn will change into abundance after you've done the work.

The fish tail of Capricorn's sea goat symbolizes emotion. There is a highly sensitive side of Capricorn that seems to be lost in this age of overachievers. Don't think that you Capricorns aren't emotional; if you hold your emotions in too long, there will be a flood that can overwhelm you.

Capricorn is the ruler of high places; think of all the pictures you've seen of goats slowly climbing a mountain. There are many mountains in sacred places that symbolize spiritual attainment. It was Mount Ararat in what is today called Iran that Noah saw peeking out of the water after the flood. Mount Nebo, also in the Ararat Mountains, was the mountain Moses looked at when God let him see the promised land. Mount Kalas in Tibet is where the god Shiva lives. Capricorns all have their own mountain to climb and there is nothing that will keep them from it.

The good news is, when you make a conscious effort to get in touch with your emotions, your ambitions fall into perspective and you are capable of maintaining a relationship with sensitivity and passion.

Everything you do is expressed through conscientious effort. You are patient and work hard at self-disciplined action. This isn't so bad really; your natural patience for the feelings of others and a desire for unconditional love builds a relationship that lasts. Perhaps Capricorn, with its cool reserve, isn't the most romantic of the signs, but you do have the ability to sustain a good relationship and a deep love that continues to grow for a lifetime.

Many of you Capricorns have learned to put aside your emotional life to attain a good position. Capricorns put off marriage and often don't date very much until their late thirties. That doesn't mean that it's impossible to mate earlier. Fate often plays a hand in relationships and they will happen when destiny decides. What you will find out is that putting off a relationship can be a form of self-delusion. Two heads are better than one, and besides, you can't work *all* the time. A Capricorn success is a continuing cycle. Even if you slide down the mountain for a while you can always turn it around and move upward again. Trust yourself; you know how dependable you are.

When you finally come to understand that no one is an island, it is possible to move into a relationship with someone that is right for you. Until that time, by blowing off marriage and just looking for uncommitted love and sex, there is a danger of separating yourself emotionally and mentally—becoming cold-hearted, irritable, and timid in action, with the mind ruling the heart too completely. That isn't the way it has to be.

Your Nature Is Earthy and Practical

In the zodiac the earth element is symbolic of the physical senses and material forms.

Earth correlates with the function of sensation. The common means of survival on the earth, like making a living, supplying basic needs, and persistently pursuing a goal, are your cup of tea. Where you get off track is by not listening to your intuition and not allowing creative concepts to manifest. You have a sensual nature and when you listen to the subtleties you can be a great psychic. But yours is not the airy-fairy type of divination. It has to be information that can be used. When you listen to your heart you can build something lasting and noble, but what good is it to be alone with your achievements?

Each of the elements have various qualities that need to be overcome for spiritual progress: air with greed, water with passion, fire with anger, and earth with attachment. To overcome attachment Capricorns must learn to serve a situation without ego gratification. Then and only then can they receive the honors they so rightly deserve.

You can get emotionally dry without opening up to the other elements. Water signs are particularly good for you. You are equipped for the water; remember your fish tail. You have to watch out or you'll have a narrow outlook and an addiction to routine and order. Love is a feeling and you can be so busy sorting everything out that you miss out on the true goal of your life, which is to create a safe home with a partner, for your family, children, pets, and all that a home entails. Classically Capricorn is the sign of the father, whose duty is to embody trust and safety. Even Capricorn women have the masculine attribute of taking concrete action.

As an earth sign you identify with your body. Gyms are full of Capricorns. But it has to be a quick fix because you don't have that much time for play. Let's face it, you think you're old, you don't know how to be a child. After living half of your life as an old man (women can be old men too) you finally wake up and get young. By the time real old age comes it doesn't bother you at all. You've been there, done that, and you're ready for love and romance. The problem is you're taking a chance; sometimes the body is tired and can't keep up. However, I know a Capricorn man who married his second wife at seventy-six years of age and quit his job. For the first time in his adult life he didn't work. That's love for you; he finally allowed himself to be smitten. It can happen earlier if you're open to risk. It's not your best trait, but it's necessary for love.

Relating on a Soul Level

Since Capricorn is the father your natural partner is Cancer, the mother.

When the amorphous beings that Plato spoke of descended into matter and separated into an earthly form. The natural pull of the yin and yang formed male and female bodies. Earth and water are naturally attracted to each other. There is always a longing to reunite with your opposite element. Being a Capricorn you have an open door into Cancer, a water sign that is deeply sensitive and emotional. The balancing of these two signs is very helpful to Capricorn because it is in the emotions, which Cancer rules, where your karma lies. This isn't to say that you must mate with a water sign. You need to seek out the attributes of Cancer in your own life before a relationship will work. In this new age we are not held to past compatibilities and you can learn to be with any sign happily.

There is an underlying principle of wanting to be in a bonded relationship for all of us that comes from the separation of one soul into two. It takes two to tango. Don't forget, with so much ambition you can overlook your soul's longing to have an inner marriage of the male and female. After this inner couple comes together you are better equipped to find happiness in a real commitment.

To truly be happy you must make the effort necessary to move toward your soul. You must ask yourself questions about what you want to create that is good and lasting in a deeper vein. There is a danger of circling around in the same groove for lifetime after lifetime, taking the same painful archetype of this life into the next.

The five-sensory logic you are so gifted with is locked in the material world. It originates in the mind. This is well and good, but the higher order of logic and true understanding comes from the heart. There is only one way to the heart and that is through the feelings. No matter how you think and what your intentions are you have no control over much that happens in your life. This is a humbling thought and one you need to take to heart. The pursuit of external power leads to repression of the emotions. Many corporations of the world are ruthless and do not give any credibility to the human condition. Heads roll every day to serve the greed and hard-hearted attitude of big industry. People that make billions are often greedy and want more. The law of Capricorn is: What goes up the mountain of success in the material world must eventually come down. Just like the unstable earth, events are always shifting. Perhaps that is why Capricorns have a tendency to worry. You know how fleeting time is and you feel you must make the most of it. The only stability we have is in our hearts.

How you move past the limitations of five-sensory perception is up to you. Seek it out, there is much information available at all times to move into the subtleties of the heart. You will become a multisensory personality who sees a new dimension of wholeness that must be felt not seen. Every time you feel negative about your life, stop—acknowledge your fear. Ask your inner self what you are feeling and what is the root of it. Monitor your response, ask your inner self what is going on. This is where wonder starts to work in your life. *Your inner self will answer.* After some trial and error you will begin to trust yourself; that brings the greatest joy. Then you will have confidence in yourself, and your real intentions will start to work in your life—not the intentions of others, but your own pure, heartfelt desires of what's best for you and all concerned.

When this happens, your mind is at home in your heart and you are a creator in the heart of God. The Ten Commandments were written for man from the perspective of the mind. When you are heart centered they are stated differently. It isn't, Thou shalt not kill. It's, Thou cannot kill. This high level of spiritual understanding is ruled by Capricorn.

Capricorn is the sign that rules Avatar (great Beings.) Jesus' birthday is celebrated in the time of Capricorn at the Saturnalia. There is deep meaning there. No matter how hard your life seems, and Capricorns always choose a difficult path, you have the inner grace to succeed.

There is no sign happier than Capricorn when she finds someone she can love and cherish. A home is right next to career and fame in your book, and you Capricorns make wonderful parents if you can control the work addiction.

Blocking Yourself from Love

Don't fool yourself; you have the same deep feelings and needs that all the other signs have.

Being born with precocious ways, you were easily programmed as a child to do *the right thing*. You don't like to make mistakes, you want to be as sure as you can. One of the goals of Capricorn is to be safe by making logical decisions. By being cautious you save yourself a lot of pain. On the other side you may be too hesitant and lose out on what you want.

In your early years you perceived a rejecting environment where you were expected to conform to a parental value system. Even though your family may look okay on the outside, it's the parents' unconscious that exerts such a powerful influence on the child. Your parents' fears and anxieties are impressed on your subconscious. I'm not a parent basher, and whether this dysfunction is literally true or not in a physical sense is not relevant; it felt that way to you at a deep level. Maybe your siblings don't feel the same way at all; maybe past-life memories color your thinking. Perhaps it is Saturn, your ruler, that rides hard on you. Whatever it is, you were trying to be an adult when you were a child. This causes you to feel helpless and worry needlessly. When you reach forty you naturally move into the power period of your life and it's easier to let go of your emotionally arrested behavior. You can re-create a new self-image that is free of the conformity and barrenness of childhood.

Here are three deep-seated issues that hold you back from the love you want:

1. You learned to repress your thoughts and feelings to please your environment, and there is an underlying fear of rejection for being wrong. Often because you were trying so hard to be an adult, your childhood was lost and the playful fun that a relationship needs isn't something you are comfortable with. This changes when you move past self-accepting to life-accepting.

2. You always want to be *right* or in the *right place* with the *right things*. This inner need to control keeps you from spontaneity and the fun of just being yourself. This is very limiting to your partner and can ruin a relationship even before it gets started.

3. In severe cases you attract someone as emotionally frozen as you are or someone you can teach, where you have the upper hand.

Deep within, you are a warm, emotional, caring, and sensual person who likes to have fun and romance as much as anyone else. As you learn to find the positive reinforcement without critical judgment you can have the love you want. There are loving people you can trust and allow into your life. After you've developed enough self-confidence and unlocked your feelings, your natural warmth, depth, and loving nature will blossom. You can learn how to play. Your gift of magnetism will radiate an earthy sensuality and you will attract love.

You are naturally monogamous. A commitment is very important to you. Oddly, although Capricorns have a tendency to be uptight, when you are open and physically attracted to a person you are intensely sexual and passionate.

You are naturally late bloomers, but a healing can be speeded up as you learn how to transform your fears, which are really only frozen feelings. Whenever you find yourself shut down, fearful, and confused, just know that these feelings precede a decision that, while not easy, is not impossible. Ask yourself, "Is that feeling really me?" Say to yourself, "This is not who I am." Take a big breath and give it a little time. Your deep inner knowing will give you the correct answer and you'll move forward with grace and comfort. Your friends and loved ones will be patient. With renewed faith in your worthiness of all that is good, you can receive the rewards of all that hard work.

A Capricorn Love Story

This is a success story in the world today.

Once upon a time there was a young man who was so intent on being the best musician in the world that he spent all his time writing, singing, and playing music. He was happy. Because he had so much talent, or maybe because he was lucky, he was "discovered" and became very famous—almost overnight. All of a sudden his long nights of hard work paid off—he had money and power. His childhood girlfriend traveled all over the world with him and he eventually married her. Everything looked great on the outside. He was on the cover of magazines, on TV, won awards, but something was missing. He had created an image that took all of his energy to keep up. Trying to keep up is draining and exhausting. Next came the children, the big house, but then the traveling started. He worked 350 days of the year. It's easy to overwork when what you do is what you love, and Capricorns can't do any work well that they don't love and celebrate.

Their work is their hobby. The rest of the story is predictable. The wife stayed home with the children, and slowly his child-hood sweetheart who he loved so dearly drifted away from him. They both changed. There was no time to share their new ideas.

Then the unbelievable happened. There were hard times; the company he was with folded; there was some scandal; his wife wanted a divorce; and to top it all, his voice was dam-aged from too much performing. He never dreamed that this would happen. He was a good person; he spent long hours wondering why these things had happened to him.

When the commercial world gives you abundance, then you are tested. A Capricorn always has a bout with rising and falling. It is part of your archetype. There is an old saying, "The higher you go (on the mountain) the farther you fall." Keep your feet on the ground of reality and don't fall for the hype. The world is capricious with celebrities. Fans tire easily and look for the new, different, and exciting. To keep up with the changes is very difficult. A new group of fans comes out every generation and they may not like your flavor of ice cream. Capricorn rules the law of plenty on earth. Our musi-cian was forced to drop back down and to rethink his life. It took a long time to reevaluate where he was and renew his broken heart. The joy he had in music dried up for a while, so he could get in touch with his inner self.

Several years later after much soul searching his natural joy in life returned as he rejoined his wife and a baby was born. He changed his lifestyle and started to discipline his work time. Then he had a phone call. He was offered a new record deal and a chance to start over, a sadder but wiser man. Now he really had it all. He knew how to make bound-aries in his life so he could enjoy the gifts he had been given.

As a Capricorn you must remember that Saturn, your ruler, makes you pay. When you lose the grounded values you were born with, trying to please the world and without con-sideration for your loved ones, it will all come tumbling down. Still, Saturn in all fairness gives you what you're due. The experience you've had of succeeding is not lost. It is still there to carry you forward to a more realistic and satisfying place. There's nothing wrong with career and fame. It's how you work with it that counts.

Don't wait until you are confused and angry to choose love. It's waiting for you to wake up and see that it will be given to you if you ask.

Your Most Authentic Self

Capricorns are complicated, or are they?

As an earth sign your nature is passive and your gift is common sense. When earth becomes active it is in the form of an avalanche or an earthquake; it can be a traitor to its own nature. There is an old saying: Don't build your house on grains of sand. However, if you start looking around for true safety, you'll find there's no such place. The earth itself always seems to have unstable environments no matter where you are, whether it's the shifting earth or the weather conditions. Scientists, by digging miles into the Antarctic, were able to uncover millions of years of weather patterns. They judged from the layers of dirt and snow that the earth, as ancient as it is, has only been inhabitable for the last ten thousand years. What we take for granted in safety on earth has never been there. You can't take anything for granted. By realizing that each day is important and having gratitude for the chance to live and grow, your life improves. Capricorn has to release the future and live in the present to make good value judgments. Creating a good package is okay in business, but love isn't created. You have to walk the path of the unknown and *allow* love to grow.

Saturn, your ruler, embodies stability. As a Capricorn you excel at bringing what is vague and unformed into manifestation. The contraction and concentration needed to create something solid is innate to you. It's getting a relationship started that is your hang-up. The act of harvesting, which is your province, implies a lot of hard work. Love doesn't have to be work—that can be your biggest surprise—and the necessary steps of courtship and commitment are easy for you, as you like to have guidelines to follow.

Aquarius in Love

ELEMENT:	Air
QUALITY:	Fixed
PLANET:	Uranus
STONE:	Amethyst
COLOR:	Lapis lazuli
ANIMAL:	Zebra
FLOWER:	Orchid
LOVE WORDS:	We are the world!

Gift — Excitement
Challenge — Unpredictability

When an Aquarius Falls in Love

The universe is in perfect order.

It's fun to find out the Sun signs of famous people and see how they exemplify them. Aquarius is the sign of great humanitarians, eccentrics, and geniuses. Many famous scientists, like Galileo and Charles Darwin, are Aquarian. As an astrologer, I love the fact that the father of electricity, Thomas Edison, was an Aquarian. Other perfectly appropriate Aquarians and great humanitarians were Abraham Lincoln, Franklin Delano Roosevelt, and Ronald Reagan—all presidents of the United States in times of great turmoil and change. Their far-reaching ideas are still affecting us today. Many great eccentrics and original artists are Aquarian, such as Wolfgang Amadeus Mozart and Jackson Pollack. Oprah Winfrey, another appropriate, stimulating, and original Aquarian, has pulled out all the stops on the television screen. With her own sense of universality and her winning ways, everyone in the world knows Oprah.

As smart and talented as you are, it's not easy for you to be intimate. The very essence of your nature is impersonal. Your sign rules groups, not individuals. Often Aquarians will have some form of separation in their marriages. One partner may live in another city, or just in a different home. There often is an unusual type of commitment. Perhaps you travel in business, you have to have your own room to sleep, or you have another living space away from family to do your work. It seems to work for you to be in your own space, and you have to admit the success of your relationship is that you and your partner are frequently apart.

A relationship can be created any way you like, as long as you can relate to each other in a sensible and equally respectful way. By knowing yourself and your partner in a deeper way, you will begin to inch along the path of love and have a wonderful relationship. With your nature, decisions are made quickly but it takes a long time to install the new condition.

You're not recognized as a romantic; your opposite sign, Leo, gets the glory in that department. Still there is none as truly loyal to love and all that it entails as you. Aquarians are primarily mental. With your quick mind and ability to see through into the crux of the matter you have a wonderful wit, and many of you are good at writing down your thoughts in a way that stimulates as well as informs. You are talented at analyzing future trends or assessing the past to design a new strategy. You feel more comfortable with someone who has a good mind who doesn't make too many emotional demands.

You don't give up easily when it comes to commitments. The perfect scenario for you is to marry your childhood sweetheart and slowly build a life together of such deep commitment that all the stress and destruction of the world doesn't pierce your seal of bondedness. In a world where 60 percent of marriages fail, this doesn't happen very often. Life isn't something you can square off and put in a box. Oddly, since Aquarius is the sign that rules electricity and electrical equipment, televisions, computers, tape recorders, appliances, and even telephones are all packaged in boxes.

Your Nature Is Airy and Thoughtful

You are a thinker, Aquarius, and your delight is to find a partner with a balanced intellectual competence to share ideas with.

You are capable of great objectivity. You love conjecture. You're often a theoretical thinker, but you're not a big risk taker in relationships. You might lead a revolution but your personal feelings are tucked inside for you alone.

As thinkers, you can be very opinionated. You have taken the time to look up the information needed on the subject. You have an excellent memory, you're well informed, and you don't bear fools lightly. You are a humanitarian and sometimes can't see the trees for the forest. People outside the home may get more from you emotionally than your loved one.

On a practical level, Aquarians are good with marketing. You can see trends and easily decipher abstract information. The fields of politics, advertising, medicine, and science are open to your excellent mind. You want the best for everyone, and it is a major desire of all Aquarians to do something that will help others. Your mind is good at processing facts, but your self-restraint puts you in situations where your needs are overlooked. Thinker types need to step over into their opposite function of feeling. When you are stuck in your mind without knowing your inner needs or feelings your mind becomes dry.

You are interested in romance, but when it comes to actually putting yourself in a vulnerable situation you hang back. When you find yourself in an emotional dilemma, ask yourself, "How do I feel?" Then follow that feeling on back as far as you can in your life and see when you first started to shut down emotionally. It may confuse you at first, but this self-analysis helps to hold you in check long enough to own your feelings. Then the next step is actually communicating them to your partner. When it comes to baring your soul, it's like you're on the wrong channel or part of your software is missing. Ask yourself how you think and there is an instant response. It takes effort to rechannel your mental energy through the heart. Yet that is where your power is.

Aquarians get along with all types. You have a very good nature and believe that everyone has the right to their own lifestyle. Live and let live is your motto, but we're talking about love and courtship here. To have better luck in that area you must broaden your experience of life, develop your own feelings and sensing nature. Many Aquarians marry their opposite sign, Leo. You are naturally attracted to their fun-loving lifestyle. Other fire signs are stimulating for you, too, they make your life more enjoyable. You are a great help to them, with your knowledge and resourcefulness. It is what they need.

We're not trying to make you into something you're not. Carl Jung says that we must integrate our opposite function (feeling) before we have any hope of integrating the intuition and the sensing function. The more harmonized you are, the more you live a life of peace and share your life with like-minded others. A reading of your natal chart will help with this information. At any rate no matter how integrated you are as an air sign you like to get as much information as you can and talk it over with other cerebral co-hearts.

Relating on a Soul Level

Spiritual creation is always a response to a need. Form follows thought.

Prometheus is the man in the symbol of Aquarius, pouring heavenly waters down to mankind. This is why Aquarius is often mistaken for a water sign. Prometheus was the divine rebel of Mount Olympus and instigated the creative power of human will. He stole fire from the gods. This is like stealing Microsoft and giving it away *free* to the whole world. The computer gods would be very angry.

You have to study mythology to understand Prometheus. He was a Titan, from a race of giants. His father was Uranus (sky god) and his mother (earth mother) was Gaia. He was a great scientist and it is said that he fashioned the first humans out of clay and breathed his vital godlike breath into them. (Perhaps he genetically engineered the human race, which doesn't sound as far-fetched as it once did.) Understandably, he had an affinity for humans, and as the story goes, he stole the fire so they could cook and warm themselves.

Jupiter was terribly angry to think that lowly mankind would have the pleasures of the gods and also be capable of godlike wisdom. To punish Prometheus, he chained him to a rock and let an eagle eat his liver—for eternity. Finally he was released from torment by his friend Chiron. Chiron, a Christ-like figure, selflessly took his place. Both Prometheus and Chiron are rulers of the new age of Aquarius that is rapidly opening in this new millennium. With this new age prevailing, perhaps Prometheus will send down more heavenly waters to heal our souls. Perhaps the fire of survival will be moved into a greater love for mankind. Prometheus is no longer bound and it has been said many times in many great spiritual traditions that we are gods.

The asteroid, Chiron, in the chart symbolizes detoxification and healing. If we purify our minds and bodies, we are being given a chance to go to the sixth dimension. This is another dimension, above the fourth and fifth where we operate now, that is made of finer energy and where subtleties are obvious to a whole-brained (use of both right and left meridians) human. The fire of true love will be understood. In thirty years who knows what amazing things we will see.

With your Promethean soul you have a lot to offer. Your genuine interest in others is a great complement to your quiet magnetism. Some Aquarians are introverted; some aren't. But what you will always find in yourself and other Aquarians is the desire to join with like-minded people and create a group energy that radiates out to a larger audience and circles the world. Like your opposite sign, Leo, you like to think big.

You need to do something important for humankind. This is how you open your heart. Your motto is that happiness comes from helping others. When this ability is developed and you connect with your soul, you are instantly connected to all the other souls and great beings in the universe. Your DNA code vibrates with theirs. Much information that is beyond our normal comprehension will be channeled in and you have the fire in the mind that is capable of doing it.

Aquarius rules the study of metaphysics, which means "beyond nature." Astrology is a way of looking beyond with the study of planetary symbols. The twelve signs of the zodiac give a blueprint of the universe, containing in essence the totality of all possible experience. In the new age the study of probabilities will go to a new level. Aquarius rules the function of distribution. We will be able to see connections that we weren't consciously aware of in times past.

The near conscious, which is closer to the conscious and not as deep as the subconscious, will be developed. In the past we have called this phenomenon a *Freudian slip*. This deeper level of the mind will be a part of our normal understanding. To take advantage of this ability the right brain will have to be appreciated and integrated with the left. Aquarius rules whole-brained function, yet you can be the most narrow-minded people when you operate out of anxiety and fear. There is no one more stubborn and opinionated than an Aquarian and no one more soulful in intention.

Through this enlarged way of being we can become more conscious. Our lessons in life will be made obvious to us through our connection to our very souls. More people will seek out real spiritual truths. The superficial moods or emotions of our society and its patterns of thinking that have held us down for thousands of years can evolve into hope of oneness and a true love for mankind. We will communicate with respect and truth. We have to.

Blocking Yourself from Love

All air signs are signs of relationship. Where would you be all by yourself?

There would be no one to bounce ideas off, no new information to sort out and classify, each thing in its perfect category—just like a human computer. You have the power that springs from knowledge. You are dedicated to truth and recognize instinctively that all humans are divinely connected. So why do you block yourself from all these wonderful gifts?

Aquarians are full of dichotomies. Your challenge is unpredictability. Although Aquarius rules freedom of mind and speech, your nature seeks out a predetermined set of conditions then imbibes it with an original pattern. Whereas Pisces is totally free of boundaries, Aquarius needs them to bounce from. There is no revolution without a change of structure, yet you are distraught by the responsibility of making choices and find it a burden to move to a new space.

You don't like surprises. You like to have a routine that is comforting to you, one you can count on. In fact, when times of change inevitably come (after all your ruler is Uranus, the planet of sudden upheavals), it takes you a while to adjust.

As strong as your commitment to love is, you have an impersonal approach that often leaves your loved one feeling left out and unappreciated. An Aquarian's mind works so fast and is so good with probabilities that a complete scene is played out in your own mind and you take it for granted that your partner is with you in this process. You are surprised when your significant other makes emotional demands. You take a lot for granted. In *your* mind it's a done deal, no use talking about it. To be in a relationship that continues to grow you need to pull those love words down from the mind, into the heart, and out of your mouth. Remember, it only takes three seconds to say "I love you."

Aquarians are very passionate people. There is nothing wrong with your libido and you're not unresponsive physically. Detachment is natural to you and love play isn't. If you tell someone you love him, you might not feel the need to repeat yourself for a long time. Not because you don't love him, but because you have already told him so.

Don't be afraid of your emotions. The water poured from heaven was the emotional feeling that is necessary for individuality. Our emotions are who we are. Before Prometheus and the stolen fire, humans were a group soul. His compassion was so great that he gave us the freedom to be out there emotionally and claim our souls. You are Prometheus's breath and you are human. Your emotional muscles may be weak but with a good workout they develop strength.

An Aquarian Love Story

You always have a deep consideration and respect for the other people.

Actor Robert Wagner is the perfect movie star, a wonderful man, and a good example of an Aquarian. He has the good nature and good looks so many Aquarians enjoy. Other

Aquarians include Paul Newman, Vanessa Redgrave, James Dean, and Jack Lemmon. What is hidden deep inside in their personal lives can be brought out on the stage and left there. The immediacy of acting brings the power in and opens the door to the freedom you so desire. It takes guts to be an actor, to reveal your soul and allow others—people you don't know and never will—to see your vulnerability. It's been said that the payoff of being out there is that it's when you're the most alive.

Many Aquarians marry young. They're old for their years in so many ways and they want autonomy from their families as soon as possible. A lot of times these early marriages don't work out. As we all know marriage is hard work; the pressure builds up, and Aquarians shut down when pressured. They want to go back to being single, to be young again. This is pretty much Wagner's story. He married Natalie Wood when they were too young and very influenced by the studio. After a divorce and another marriage he was single again and so was Natalie. They went back together for the second time and it worked, until her untimely death. Aquarians, being ruled by Uranus, always seem to have at least one real tragedy in their lives. Wagner raised his three daughters by himself and slowly began to rebuild his life. He started dating a friend, Jill St. John (Aquarius rules friendships), and married her many years later.

Wagner's career has continued to grow. If you look at his pictures when he was young he was exceedingly handsome and had a twinkle in his eye. Now in his sixties he is just as handsome, with the same old twinkle, but much more shows in his eyes. There is a softer look, one of a person who has mellowed with life. He is a compassionate person, his presence is uplifting, and it is very apparent that he is in touch with his emotions. He's had heartbreak and many upsets and he came through with flying colors. It's rare to find a balanced movie star and nice to know that fame and notoriety don't have to continue to take their toll.

Your Most Authentic Self

You have an instinctive knowledge of the necessity to maintain integrity and how to conform to an accepted pattern for the sake of communal well-being.

Aquarius is the sign of friends. You have great personal charisma but you stand back and observe a great deal of the time. The fact is you like autonomy. If a social gathering includes people you're comfortable with, you can enjoy yourself. If only strangers are present, you're likely to stand apart and sneak out as soon as you can. I think this is because you are an air sign, which rules the space between, separate but equal, and not the connecting point. Although you are social you are also antisocial.

With this detached manner one wonders how you ever make a contact that leads to love. This isn't a problem; people are drawn to you, and with a flash of insight so typical of your sign you seem to know at first glance if something is there. You might wait awhile, then make a move at the right time. You are hesitant at first, but when you're ready there's no stopping you.

The essence of your sign is love. There is a transcendent quality to your very being. You enter into the higher levels of consciousness naturally. You have the X-ray vision of Superman. You sense the truth and divine the true nature of whoever stands before you.

One word of advice for Aquarius. Inside you are always slightly urgent. Maybe because your ideas come so fast or because your body energy is stepped up more than others. This verve never goes completely away, so you need time alone. Alone time suits your thoughtful nature, but you shouldn't neglect your loved ones. Allow yourself to be nourished by others. Too much isolation is your enemy.

Your duty in life is to be in harmony with others and uphold the highest level of service for mankind. This can be done by being a good parent, by being conscientious in your work, and by opening your heart to your life mate. After this, you will be a light to many. You are a very powerful person and deep inside you know it. You have the power of originality and humanitarianism.

Dane Rudhyar, a great astrologer, wrote in his book *The Illuminated Way* a message for all of us. We all have Aquarius in our chart somewhere.

Power is not to be clung to, and neither is love. Power is to be used. Love is to be used. Life is to be used. All that is ours to touch, to feel, to experience is to be used, to be managed. It must be managed to serve a purpose that is true, real, divine—simply because it is evolutionary purpose that alone makes sense. Nothing makes sense which does not go forward in greater, deeper, nobler, more inclusive creative activity; and all motion forward demands that power be summoned, used, and managed.

There is only one purpose for your power and that is for peace. The power of truth, which is your birthright, can be maintained by cultivating a genuine openness to things as they really are. The power to perceive the truth in your partner's argument is essential to achieving the bonded relationship you so desire. Truth is something to which all people naturally respond. Your truth attracts the truth in others.

February 19–March 20

Pisces in Love

ELEMENT:	Water
QUALITY:	Mutable
PLANET:	Neptune
STONE:	Aquamarine
COLOR:	Sea blue
ANIMAL:	Dolphin
FLOWER:	Lotus
LOVE WORDS:	Dream a little dream of me!

Gift — Sensuality
Challenge — Elusiveness

When a Pisces Falls in Love

Pisces lives in a psychic world of supersensitivity.

You are soulfully connected to other dimensions and there is a tendency to not be able to distinguish what is fantasy and what is real. Pisceans are especially visual, which is why so many of you are artists. You are gifted with a multileveled consciousness and your sensitivity goes from being extremely intuitive into the psychic. You are very tactile. When you touch something there is a stream of consciousness that feeds you information (psychometry), and you are clairaudient (hearing an inner voice), and psychic (seeing pictures in the mind) as well. You live in a world of physical and psychic sensuality.

Regretfully, in this fantasia of feelings and emotion, with myriad colors and impressions, you often see what you want to see. Like finding faces in clouds. Your emotions can color your response to the information that you pick up. In stressful situations there is a tendency to overreact. By being aware of your wonderful gifts, you can decipher the subtle information without being afraid of it.

Being ultra-sensitive can be a burden to you. In reading your partner's thoughts you have to be careful or you might pick up something you'd rather not deal with, or feel that you are infringing on your loved one's privacy. It's also important to verify this information, as your emotions can color your impression. To use your gift well you must remain sensitive as well as highly principled, and avoid the temptation to be manipulative. Building a close and tender relationship is your life's dream. By being sensitive to your partner you can develop a satisfying communication and a wonderful intimacy that other signs must struggle to attain.

In an interview Piscean Sharon Stone said that one of the main things she had learned in life was that women must be able to tell the truth. This is good advice. (Of course, this goes for men, too.) Many young people today stay so busy they build up defenses and find it hard to let a new person into their feelings. Pisces types like to please to the point of victimizing themselves. You often feel the need to say the right thing instead claiming your own thoughts. Going with the flow doesn't mean you can't confront a situation that isn't right for you. By loving too much you have a tendency to give too much. A loving, compassionate relationship does not mean saying yes all the time.

When you are in the immediacy of a stimulating moment (especially in your love life) in all its panorama of light, fantasy, and mystical feeling, you can be totally captivated and lose your ability to distinguish what is really there. You have to learn to set boundaries. It is easy for you to be captured by the drama of the moment, then later on realize that it wasn't what you thought at all. When you meet someone who seems to fit the picture of what you are seeking in a relationship, it's important for you to move very slowly. Pisces can fall in love at the drop of a hat and can fall out just as quickly.

Your Nature Is Fluid and Emotional

All water signs are in tune with the emotional aspects of life.

There are no barriers standing between you and your deep subconscious. It isn't easy to be fused with other people and feel so responsible for their happiness. Of all the water signs, Pisces is the most psychic. The other water signs are intuitive, but you go way beyond that, and you are the most physically sensitive of all the signs. You are ultra-absorbent, very like litmus paper, and your finely tuned sensitivity is constantly testing the climate of your surroundings.

Water has a great force and penetrating power. Lakes and rivers follow the flow of the land. Water is yielding but all-conquering—it is victorious over all the other elements. Water puts out fire, washes away soft earth, or winds its way around rocks. It saturates the atmosphere so that the wind dies.

Water wins by yielding. The softness of water is very deceiving; it gives way to obstacles with beguiling humility. It never attacks but continues to wind its way to the sea. We live in a world that is mostly water. Its softness cleanses our bodies, comforts our thirst, and nourishes our crops, but it also carves great canyons.

As a water sign you take on the changeable properties of this mutable element, and being so flexible, you have no real boundaries; it's easy for you to fit the shape of what others want from you. This can make you feel like a victim. If you don't have say over your own life it is a prison of your own making. No one has the right to make your decisions for you.

Choice is the biggest gift you have in life. Don't give it up so easily, thinking others know more than you.

Watery and emotional, Pisces is a sign of extremes. You have the ability to go into the fluidity of imagination. You can see into uncharted worlds of the arts and excel at poetry, dance, and acting. Virgo, an excellent partner for you, rules the technique that is needed to get these imaginings and dreams actualized. Water and your balancing element, earth, mixed together make bricks, which build lasting edifices and monuments.

Pisces, the ruler of bodies of water, is in the fourth house (the home) in my natal chart. With a water sign in this location, my soul needs simplification and serenity in my surroundings. When the good luck planet, Jupiter, transited the home area of the chart, magically, luckily, and suddenly I moved to Florida, a Piscean state. Strangely, it was the dolphins (ruled by Pisces) that brought me down here from New York City. I came to this area to swim with the wild dolphins. As I write this book, I'm looking at the Gulf of Mexico where the dolphins swim by daily. So beautiful and calming, I find my creativity is better around the water, it comforts my Capricorn soul.

As a Pisces you are connected to a great sense of oneness. Pisces is the sign of the soul. With your sensitive nature you need to explore yourself, and to fulfill your potential you must learn the language of your subconscious. So much of your perception is subliminal and you are influenced by outside events more than you can know rationally. When this is a positive situation, it's a great gift and blessing, and you're able to help others with heightened awareness. Edgar Cayce, the greatest psychic of the twentieth century, was a Pisces. Interestingly, the Institute of Enlightenment is in Virginia Beach, Virginia, a Virgo place. Pisces need the support of earth polarity to function at their highest.

Pisces is the most feminine of all the signs. I call it the sign of yin yin, as Aries is the sign of yang yang. Pisces is almost totally right-brained. Information comes to you from all levels in a divergent way. I once saw a man with only the use of his right brain do a painting. His face was pressed so close to the paper he couldn't see it and yet he drew an incredibly beautiful and very accurate picture. This was done without any of the organizational skills one would think were necessary to do an accurate rendering. It actually looked like it was being run off a printer. When he finished, it was complete; his paintings were exactly perfect in perception and beautiful in every way. They had come from another dimension of the mind that sees thing differently. He saw no beginning, middle, or end—he was exactly in the moment and painted each piece of information as it came. I found that very reassuring. There is a wise part inside of us that sees things from a holistic viewpoint, against all logic, not as we've been taught to see—with one thing leading to another. This man touched upon truth at a level so deep, it was beyond rationality.

We have full use of our brains if we so choose. As a Pisces you were born with a highly developed right brain; you are able to reach into the greatest creative energy available. It is your gift, but it can delude you. You must keep a reality check going in your mind's eye, and as Sharon Stone has learned, be able to tell the truth. You are a truth seeker. The next step is comforting your fears of rejection, which come out of the deep subconscious. You Pisceans can be very courageous in that you know deep within that courage is not the absence of fear—but rather the belief that something exists that is greater than fear.

1994 Inaugural Speech of Nelson Mandela

Our deepest fear is not that we are inadequate. Our deepest fear is that we are powerful beyond measure. It is our light, not our darkness, that most frightens us. We ask ourselves, "Who am I to be brilliant, gorgeous, talented, and fabulous?" Actually, who are you not to be? You are a child of God, your playing small doesn't serve the world. There is nothing enlightening about shrinking so that other people won't feel insecure around you. We were born to make manifest the glory of God that is within us. It is not just in some of us: it's in everyone. And as we let our own light shine, we unconsciously give other people permission to do the same. As we are liberated from our own fears, our presence automatically liberates others.

The greatest need of the Piscean temperament is the capability to endure. There is an element of restlessness that must be conquered. When you learn how to open to your soul, you are thrice blessed; body, mind, and soul are three names for the same love principle. You are deeply connected to your inner essence by your very nature, yet you are very physical. Being soul connected doesn't cancel out the ability to be imaginatively sensual. In a relationship you have much to offer, especially after you've allowed your subtle energy to connect with your partner.

As a liquid element you are looking for someone or something else to concretize your fluidity. This can be a person, a job, or a group force. This feeling of dependency can cause you to feel urgent and helpless in complex situations. You need to have a checklist of practical assessments to help you make your own decisions in confusing situations when you need a level head. It's better if you sort things out yourself and find a sense of inner stability.

Dependency is its own reward. You might have the support of someone else, but if your reliance is too strong, your mind and body go lax, and your life is controlled by someone else. You are a prisoner of your own lack of backbone. A message from your symbolic ruler, the fish, would be that fish have scales of protection and a strong backbone.

You must not be a victim of your vulnerability. You need defenses. Even the beautiful rose has thorns. Remember the greatest gift a Pisces is given in life is courage. Take what you are afraid of out of your subconscious so it can be seen. Then you know what to conquer.

You have the ability to tolerate and learn from your life struggles and you can move out of a helpless state of confusion and stagnation into great serenity.

With consideration for others, dedication to beneficial projects, and learning how to make definite boundaries, you are boosted into positive and productive dimensions of living. It is not selfish for you to be healthier, wealthier, and more fulfilled in life; when you help yourself, you help the world. Your hard-won battle over victimization brings a sense of well-being with all its outer manifestations. This abundance releases more light into the race consciousness for the benefit of all.

Blocking Yourself from Love

In your intimate relationships you are naturally a giving person.

You are highly sensitive and vulnerable, reflecting a natural kind of innocence and naiveté. You are a romantic and hopelessly in love with love. With your dreamy ways, you easily fall into a false idea of what love is. Rather than having the patience to develop a relationship with real intimacy and commitment you jump into extremely exciting scenarios, without much forethought. You form relationships that rarely correlate to the ideal mate that you consciously or unconsciously desire and really deserve. You often settle for less, picking someone beneath you socially or people that have serious emotional problems. You rationalize your choice by thinking your partner is really good inside or that he will change—if you love him enough. Inside you know the truth.

You can hold on to your fantasy only so long before the truth will come out and you become totally disillusioned. If someone on your level comes in, you hide because there is a deep fear that if they knew you they wouldn't love you.

The most important lesson a Pisces has is not to be a victim. With your self-depreciating attitude you can find a reason to be unhappy at every turn. Your love life can be a constant drama and you can set yourself up to be on the losing end with your helpless perspective. You must learn how to take the risk of being hurt, which is underneath every love choice, and still live with an open heart. Sorry, there are never any guarantees.

The depression brought on by impossible relationships can lead to a broken heart and a feeling of rejection so deep that it triggers all your fears of being unworthy of love. You can drown your sorrows in addictive behaviors, such as drugs and alcohol, compulsive habits like eating disorders and sex addiction—the list goes on. Even the Internet can be addictive.

It doesn't have to be that way. You deserve the best. Jupiter, the planet of abundance and good luck, is the subruler of Pisces. The blessings and the grace are there waiting for you to see. With a mature attitude that accepts your wonderful attributes you can discriminate between reality and illusion.

When you are in a relationship there is a desire to throw yourself into your partner's arms and blend into his world, leaving yours behind. You are in conflict within yourself, trying to escape into the joy of lovemaking but all the time analyzing the situation. You become a victim of your own indecision. Because of this vacillation you are prone to escape. Many Pisces fall in love very quickly, or think they do, and marry as soon as possible, thinking that their love is above the normal problems of life. Later when the fantasy is over you find that couldn't be further from the truth. This is the reason that Pisceans have the reputation of being married the most, except for Cancer (who runs a close second). Both are sensitive water signs trying to find love in all the wrong places.

There is a tendency toward emotional instability that gives you a predisposition to play out other people's dramas. Just like a sponge you absorb their feelings and think they're your own. Later you wonder why you felt so strongly about something that doesn't pertain to you and that is not even your business. You need quiet time and a strong sense of self to filter through the many impressions that come from your environment.

As you learn to allow the practical sensibilities of your opposite sign, Virgo, to function, your love life greatly improves. Courtship and marriage are much more Virgoan than Piscean. Even though a Virgo can choose to live alone, the true nature of Virgo is in a home with bread baking in the oven and children playing in a well-trimmed yard. Of the opposites signs there are none as different as Virgo and Pisces, and both signs need the integration of the other to enjoy life. The unity of Virgo and Pisces is the most creative combination of all the signs. Opportunity comes to those who persist in their dreams.

A Pisces Love Story

I have a Pisces client who has come to me for astrological consultation for years.

She is enchantingly beautiful, with dreamy Piscean eyes and a wonderful way of presenting herself to the world. To know her is to love her, and she's for real. But when it comes to her love life, forget it. When she did pick a partner I wondered what she was thinking.

She was the creative director for a large communications firm. She traveled all over the world and was happy with her life, except for feeling lonely. The same thing happened to her that happens to a lot of young people these days. Her lifestyle kept her single. She was out of town a lot and she hadn't had a date since her last promotion. It's hard to meet someone traveling so much, and when she was home she was tired.

Her biological clock was ticking and she became obsessed with getting married. She urgently started looking around for a mate. When she came in for a reading she was so disappointed in her last few attempts that she felt that she was a victim and there was no hope for her in the love department. Being too sensitive to others and unaware of your needs is a problem and it can cause you to shut down. You take a lot for granted and don't take the time to learn about your partner's emotional needs.

With some astrological counseling she was able to see that she was looking for a sex relationship, not a partner. She thought that being sexually attractive was a solution to her goal of getting married. Her self-esteem came from being sexy to men. When she got what she wanted and men were attracted to her, she felt like she was in control. Then she would be disappointed because they were only interested in her body. Most men start out with a sexual goal in a relationship, and if women use only their desirability as a solution to getting what they want, they will be greatly disappointed. If sex is your goal, that's exactly what you get.

She had to learn that the truly gratifying element of a relationship is intimacy. Her fear of closeness came from the lack of understanding of what a real relationship is. As a child she had been very private and hadn't learned how to share her feelings with others. Pisces rules the lost child, the child who observes and doesn't participate in emotional ways. My client wanted to win love like she achieved in work, objectively and aggressively. Real emotional contact wasn't something she was comfortable with. In fact, she was terrified of it. What if he really knew that she had a temper? That she really didn't want sex every time she saw him? That she didn't know how to communicate with a man?

Women have a higher capacity for intimacy than men. Men can be physically intimate with a woman and leave it there, while women usually have a deeper experience, so capricious attitudes about sex are a no-win for them.

The first thing I saw for my client was for her to back off of the urgent feeling of just wanting to get married. Her aspects were good for meeting someone the next spring and she had time to balance her life. Next I suggested that she not make sex step one. What really works in a relationship is to put sex after developing intimacy and trust, then comes a chance for a commitment. I suggested a decent time of dating to create a comfortable feeling of trust before she started a sex relationship. The time on this varies with each couple. No one can make that choice for you. You and I both know that sometimes it works out and intimacy comes very quickly to the couple, but you can't bet on it.

The next thing I saw as I looked at her chart was that she needed to know herself, do an inventory of what a relationship means to her and what she wanted in a relationship. Pisceans need to be prepared for commitment. If someone comes in, no matter how attractive, you need to date awhile to know what is really there.

After a personal inventory, she came to these conclusions:

1. She took responsibility for creating her life, fully aware of the consequences of her choices.

2. She learned to say no when she wanted to.

3. She no longer played the victim.

4. She started to really communicate with people— men and women alike.

These realizations made all the difference in her life. The last I heard she was dating someone who was good marriage material for her. Her aspects did bring in someone who was right for her when she learned what she needed. She's taking plenty of time, knowing her tendency to dream her life instead of live it.

Your Most Authentic Self

The traditional symbol for Pisces is two fish swimming in opposite directions. It is said these opposing forces cause insecurity and indecisiveness, even suggesting a loss of spiritual power. When I was in Egypt at the Ptolemaic Temple of Dendera (circa 100 B.C.), I saw a beautiful old zodiac on the ceiling of one of the upstairs rooms. Egyptologists think this zodiac is a copy of one much older than the temple itself. In fact the Great Precessional Age alluded to in this zodiac is the Cancerian Age, approximately ten thousand years ago. In this older zodiac the symbols for Pisces were very different; the fish are swimming in the same direction. This suggests to me that Pisces have the ability to align their dual nature, to listen to their strong inner intuition, and to use their prophetic gifts. Without self-doubt you can believe in yourself and use your gifts for the benefit of all concerned without wanting to manipulate or escape. As we enter the new great Age of Aquarius, it's time for the Piscean fish to swim heart and soul in the same direction.

You are sensitive; basically you are creative and self-sufficient. When you enter into a relationship, you must see your partner's soul. Your largess is intuition and faith; leave the tears behind. As Shakespeare says in *Romeo and Juliet:* "Venus smiles not in a house of tears."

Part IV
Soul Signs—Soul Mates

"When all the souls had chosen their lives according to their lots, they went before Lachesis. And she sent with each, as the guardian of his life and the fulfiller of his choice, the daimon (guardian angel) that he had chosen. This divinity led the soul first to Clotho, under her hand and the turning of the spindle to ratify the destiny of his lot and choice, and after contact with her, the daimon again led the soul to the spinning of Atropos to make the web of its destiny irreversible, and then without a backward look it passed beneath the throne of necessity."

—Plato, the myth of Er, from *The Republic*

The Myth of Er

Plato says a lot here that is significant to understanding the concept of our soul's transformation into human form. The point is that life is a series of choices made before we are born.

The Myth of Er suggests that your soul chooses the life you want to experience and chooses a guardian angel to escort you through your human experience. A myth is always timeless. Your soul is continually in a timeless state of making selections, and since ancient psychology locates the soul with the heart, it is your heart that holds the image of your destiny.

Your angel takes you to Clothos who confirms the lot you have chosen and then empowers your choices. Atropho then compresses the multidimensionality of your soul indelibly into the pattern for your human form—like when a painter commits his idea to the canvas, that form is the shape from which the rest of the painting evolves.

The gateway of Necessity implies that you are born and start the life that has been created as inevitable and inescapable. In other words you have created your new life and now must live it out.

There is another step that is important to know about. Just before you enter human life, you pass through the plain of Lethe (forgetting) so that all the previous activities of choosing are wiped out. You forget the whole thing, although it still remains in your subconscious and your soul remembers.

It's all about choices. The concept is the same with soul mates.

Your Soul Mate

Everyone wants a soul mate, but what is that, really?

There are many theories. Most people believe that a soul mate is the *one soul* that they are compatible with in this lifetime. But I prefer to think that we meet several soul mates in life and it's our choice whether or not to continue on together. It may be your destiny to meet, but the decision to continue is up to you. Many times I read for people who have met a soul mate that is not as spiritually evolved in this lifetime and choose not to pursue the union. I am happy to reassure them in their devastation that this is not their only chance in this life to have a soulful connection.

Nothing is so fated it can't be changed. Even though we meet someone that we are destined to meet and have a soul connection with, the choice has to be made to stay together. It's worth saying again that you create your world based on the selections you make before birth and after. There are no wrong choices, every choice has a path and a karma. Each choice brings its own consequence. There are really no right or wrong decisions. We must live with an open heart no matter how great the risk of being hurt. When our hearts are open, our guardian angel, or daimon, is more available to us for guidance.

To have a good sense of our inner being, our soul, we must develop a view that is deep and penetrating, that can look between the lines and catch the images that might otherwise pass unnoticed. When love comes into the picture the soul is there serving the situation as best it can through the filters of the ego. The soul resides in the now. When we first start a relationship the passion and joy is in the now. Then out of fear the ego starts looking to the future. Is this the one? Is this my happy-ever-after? Is this my destiny? Such is the dilemma of love—how to go through all of the phases of relationship and stay present.

The outcome isn't as important as you might think. We have another level of higher consciousness called the spirit that looks over the whole picture and looks for transcendence. The soul rides out daily life, the emotional ups and downs, and keeps us connected to our spirit, that part of ourselves that is profound and wise.

As we become soul-connected and long for our soul mate, we must surrender to the way the soul works. It doesn't work well in stimulating events, the soul loves the ordinary, simple things of life. Thomas Moore in his book *Soul Mates* says that our soul doesn't like the fast pace of modern society. Intimacy is what the soul likes best, because through intimacy it is nourished and made safe.

Soul isn't interested in perfection, it wants experience. Only through living life does the soul grow through the decisions and consequences. We have to evolve in order to first recognize then bond with our soul mate. Through understanding your Sun sign and the signs of your loved ones, you can realize a deeper connection with your own soul. This deep inner wisdom opens us all to a soulful connection and the opportunity of maintaining enhanced relationships.